Archaeologists, Tourists, Interpreters

Bloomsbury Egyptology

Series Editor
Nicholas Reeves

Ancient Egyptian Technology and Innovation, Ian Shaw
Burial Customs in Ancient Egypt, Wolfram Grajetzki
Court Officials of the Egyptian Middle Kingdom, Wolfram Grajetzki
The Egyptian Oracle Project, Robyn Gillam and Jeffrey Jacobson
Hidden Hands, Stephen Quirke
The Middle Kingdom of Ancient Egypt, Wolfram Grajetzki
Performance and Drama in Ancient Egypt, Robyn Gillam

Archaeologists, Tourists, Interpreters

Exploring Egypt and the Near East in the Late 19th–Early 20th Centuries

Rachel Mairs and Maya Muratov

Bloomsbury Academic
An imprint of Bloomsbury Publishing Plc

B L O O M S B U R Y
LONDON • NEW DELHI • NEW YORK • SYDNEY

Bloomsbury Academic

An imprint of Bloomsbury Publishing Plc

50 Bedford Square	1385 Broadway
London	New York
WC1B 3DP	NY 10018
UK	USA

www.bloomsbury.com

British Library Cataloguing-in-Publication Data

A catalogue record for this book is available from the British Library.

ISBN: HB: 978-1-47258-879-1
PB: 978-1-47258-880-7
ePDF: 978-1-47258-882-1
ePub: 978-1-47258-881-4

Library of Congress Cataloging-in-Publication Data

A catalog record for this book is available from the Library of Congress.

Series: Bloomsbury Egyptology

Typeset by Fakenham Prepress Solutions, Fakenham, Norfolk NR21 8NN

To invisible interpreters.
In Memoriam, Steven Seymour, an interpreter.

Contents

List of Illustrations   ix

Acknowledgements   xi

1   Introduction: Interpreting the Orient   1

2   Mediating Language and Culture   11
    Dragomans and Tourists   11
    The Profession of Dragoman   13
    Innocents Abroad   21
    Managing Clients   27
    Learning Arabic   31

3   Archaeologists in the Field   45
    Flinders Petrie in Egypt and Palestine   45
    T. E. Lawrence in Egypt and Syria   50
    Sir Leonard Woolley   54
    Max Mallowan and Agatha Christie   64

4   Americans in the 'Land of the Bible'   73
    The Wolfe Expedition   73
    The Babylonian Expedition of the University of Pennsylvania
       1888–90: First and Second Campaigns   80

5   Daniel Z. Noorian: the 'Afterlife' of an Interpreter   91

6   Solomon Negima: A Dragoman and his Clients   105
    The Testimonial Book of Dragoman Solomon N. Negima   105
    Interpreter on the Nile   110
    Dragoman in Palestine   113
    Oxford to Palestine and *Alone Through Syria*   119
    Floyd House   125

Contents

7   Conclusion   129

References   135
Index   145

List of Illustrations

Figure 1: Postcard of Dragoman Khalil S. Gandour at the World's Fair, St. Louis, 1904. © Rachel Mairs. 5

Figure 2: Herodotus and his interpreter. From Ade 1906. 14

Figure 3: 'A Trusty Dragoman'. Vintage postcard, c. 1917. © Rachel Mairs. 18

Figure 4: 'The Dragoman who saw the Joke'. Punch, June 1937. 19

Figure 5: 'Dragoman explaining cartouches in the temple of Komombo' from Sladen 1911. 29

Figure 6: Le drogman arabe. 38

Figure 7: An extract from Khalīfah ibn Maḥmūd al-Miṣrī's Qalā'id al-jumān fī fawā'id al-tarjumān / Instructions aux drogmans (1850). 41

Figure 8: Petrie's Addenda to Baedecker's Vocabulary (1888). 47

Figure 9: '"Napoleon," our interpreter at Kastamuni', from Woolley 1921: viii. 63

Figure 10: Dragoman business cards, of various dates. Top right: Hassab, Hamad. Calling card (Cairo, Egypt). Brooklyn Museum Libraries. Wilbour Library of Egyptology. Special Collections. 92

Figure 11: Gravestone of Daniel Z. Noorian and Belle Ward Noorian, Rosedale Cemetery, Montclair, Essex County, New Jersey, USA. 93

Figure 12: Letterhead of Daniel Z. Noorian. 96

Figure 13: The Testimonial Book of Dragoman Solomon N. Negima. © Rachel Mairs. 106

Figure 14: Testimonial letter from Lord Dalrymple. © Rachel Mairs. 107

Figure 15: Photographs of Solomon Negima, from inside the back cover of his testimonial book. © Rachel Mairs. 109

Figure 16: Testimonial letter from Capt Leach. © Rachel Mairs. 111

Figure 17: Testimonial letter from Capt Teale. © Rachel Mairs. 112

Figure 18: Rev Charles T. Walker, wearing Solomon Negima's red tarboosh. Floyd 1902, 146. 118

Figure 19: Letter from D. Ford Goddard to Solomon Negima. ©
   Rachel Mairs.   119
Figure 20: Solomon Negima (front row, left) with his family and RLDS
   missionaries, at Floyd House, Jerusalem, 1912 (Braby 2008: 54).   126

Acknowledgements

This book is an offshoot of a project-in-progress on multilingualism and the complex roles of interpreters in antiquity, based on epigraphic and literary sources of the Hellenistic and Roman periods from the Northern Black Sea, Rome, Western Roman Provinces and Egypt. It began in the spring of 2008 with a series of conversations about interpreters – ancient and modern – that took place on the third floor of the Institute for the Study of the Ancient World (ISAW), New York University, where we both were Visiting Research Scholars. We are grateful to the director of ISAW, Roger Bagnall, for the opportunities provided and for creating a stimulating environment where the seeds of this venture were first sown.

This book has been a collaborative venture throughout, but each author has taken special responsibility for particular sections. Rachel Mairs prepared the introductory chapters, material on Petrie and Lawrence and the section on Solomon Negima. Maya Muratov prepared the conclusion, material on Finati and D'Athanasi, Woolley, Mallowan and Christie, American expeditions and the section on Daniel Z. Noorian. Any first person references within the text should be understood in this light, but the book's broader arguments are the product of joint research and discussion.

Among many people who have contributed to the making of this book, we would like to thank the following: Nicholas Reeves, for his encouragement of this project; Charlotte Loveridge, formerly of Bloomsbury, and Alice Reid and Anna MacDiarmid, of Bloomsbury, for their constant help with the manuscript; the anonymous reviewers for their insightful and helpful comments; James Moske and Barbara File, of the Metropolitan Museum of Art Archives, for allowing access to the Noorian files and for permission to use them in our book; Dan and Patty Baumgartner, of Rogue River Books, for information on the testimonial book of Solomon N. Negima; and the many book and antique dealers who have helped us gather dragoman ephemera, such as the postcards illustrated in this book.

More such pieces are discussed on the *Hermeneis* blog (http://hermeneis. wordpress.com/).

Our colleagues, friends and family members provided moral, intellectual or other kinds of support along the way: Arietta Papaconstantinou, our parents, Raymond and Carol Mairs and Boris and Adelaida Potapov; Cyrill Muratov; Roberta Casagrande-Kim; Tiziana d'Angelo.

This book is dedicated to the many 'invisible' interpreters whose stories are buried in the accounts of others.

Rachel Mairs and Maya Muratov
Oxford and New York, October 2014

1

Introduction

Interpreting the Orient

A brief aside in the Palestinian-American literary critic Edward W. Said's memoir *Out of Place* offers an insight into what it has meant to interpret the Middle East to Western consumers, from the nineteenth century to the present day. Said's paternal grandfather, he tells us, 'at some point in his life ... was a dragoman who because he knew German had, it was said, shown Palestine to Kaiser Wilhelm' (Said 1999: 6).[1] A dragoman was a guide and translator, engaged by foreign travellers to facilitate their journeys (Carswell 1982: 487–8).[2] On the one hand, his role was to interpret the Orient[3] for travellers whose lack of Arabic or Turkish would otherwise have made it impossible for them to interact with and understand their surroundings. On the other, his role was to protect his clients from the more inconvenient or uncomfortable aspects of travel. The employment of a dragoman enabled a foreign visitor to insulate him- or her-self from the Orient in a way which offered an illusion of engaging with it. What they came to 'know' about the Orient was mediated through the filters of their own observations and preconceptions, and their dragoman's explanations and interpretations.

European and American travellers in Egypt and the Middle East in the second part of the nineteenth century and early twentieth century, the

---

[1] This is plausible – the Kaiser travelled with a large party of dragomans and other attendants – but I have not been able to find any record of individual interpreters and their roles. The tour arrangements were made by Thomas Cook.

[2] The term 'dragoman' was used throughout the Ottoman Empire and neighbouring regions to indicate a translator, guide and mediator. There is an extensive literature on diplomatic dragomans at Constantinople in the Early Modern period (for example, Rothman 2009). Our focus, in this book, is on dragomans as guides for foreign travellers and Anglophone archaeologists in Egypt and the Levant.

[3] In the period covered by this book 'the Orient' was understood to mean the Middle East or the Far East, not exclusively the latter, as became more common in later periods. It is the term used by most of the voyagers discussed in the following chapters to refer to the area of their travels.

period covered by this book, were consumers in several senses. The act of travelling was in itself an act of conspicuous consumption, a new luxury for well-off members of the upper and middle classes. With the advent of the first Thomas Cook's package tours to the Orient in the 1860s–70s, travel in the region was, to an extent, rendered a commodity, which one might show off to one's friends and contemporaries. So many tourists of the period wrote and published accounts of their travels – some of them without either literary merit or intrinsic interest – that the genre became worthy of satire. Travellers were consumers of culture, ancient and modern, and they were a market for everything from genuine antiquities to 'tourist tat'. But they were also representatives of colonial powers, of foreign mechanisms of control which consumed the resources of the Middle East.

We have used the term 'Orient' because this is the way in which contemporary European and American travellers conceived of the Eastern Mediterranean and Middle East, as a region whose history and culture stood as an antithesis to their own. By the 1970s, the historical project of interpreting the Orient to the Occident had been recognized as inseparable from the history of Western colonial domination. Edward Said's *Orientalism* showed how Western cultural representations of the East – including the accounts of travellers without expressly political motives for their presence in the region – reproduced romanticized, exoticized images which served to justify Western colonial dominance. An example to which we shall return is that of the French novelist Gustave Flaubert's notes on his stay in Egypt (1849–50), and more specifically his account of a night spent in the company of the dancer and courtesan Kuchuk Hanem. As Said notes, Kuchuk Hanem:

> never spoke of herself, she never represented her emotions, presence, or history. *He* spoke for and represented her. He was foreign, comparatively wealthy, male, and these were historical facts of domination that allowed him not only to possess Kuchuk Hanem physically but to speak for her and tell his readers in what way she was 'typically Oriental'. (Said 1978: 6)

We are not in a position to give Kuchuk Hanem back her voice, but there are ways in which Western historical accounts of the 'Orient' and 'Orientals' can be made to yield information on the lives of their subjects from different perspectives. Recent projects such as Stephen Quirke's study of the archaeologist

Sir W. M. Flinders Petrie's Egyptian workforce show how archival materials, in particular, provide wonderful opportunities to explore the lives, professional expertise and even personalities of the apparently faceless and voiceless Oriental masses (Quirke 2010). In this book, we endeavour to do the same for the dragomans who worked for Western travellers and sojourners in Egypt and the Near East, including archaeologists. Dragomans are doubly handicapped in terms of their historical visibility: as Orientals, and as interpreters, whose role in a transaction is usually regarded – by the client – as solely one of transparent mediation, without regard for the myriad social and cultural cues which the interpreter must also translate, or choose not to (Venuti 2008). The stories which we tell in the following chapters come from different sides of the linguistic and cultural transaction between East and West. The published accounts of Western travellers and archaeologists offer a client-driven perspective on dragomans – the writer's own, and other people's. In these, for the most part, the Oriental man, in the form of the dragoman, no more speaks for himself than does the Oriental woman Kuchuk Hanem. Archival documents and photographs allow us a slightly different perspective. Sometimes, we are fortunate enough to have a dragoman's own words, or a more impartial account of his activities than that of a (sometimes disgruntled) client.

Such cases of a dragoman speaking for himself to a Western audience are, however, rare. In 1819, several decades before the period covered by this book, an Egyptian dragoman named Abraham V. Salamé published an account, in English, of his role in a British military expedition to Algiers (Salamé 1819). A lengthy and enthusiastic review in the *Literary Gazette* (276–7), of London, for that same year, dwells on certain qualities of Salamé and his narrative which later travellers in the Middle East would also see as positive qualities in their dragomans: Christian faith, respectable family, education, training in European languages and service to European colonial agents. The review concludes, however, by mocking Salamé's 'truly ridiculous' acknowledgements of the assistance and influence of a large number of illustrious Europeans. Such name-dropping was by no means unusual in contemporary books by European authors, but the anonymous reviewer takes the opportunity to mock the otherwise sophisticated Salamé as a servile Oriental.

The stories we cover in the following chapters belong to, and are told by, a range of people involved in the tourism and heritage trades in Egypt and the

Near East. Some, such as William Makepeace Thackeray, Gustave Flaubert and Agatha Christie, are well known literary figures. Famous pioneering archaeologists, including Sir W. M. Flinders Petrie, Sir Leonard Woolley and Sir Max Mallowan, also make an appearance. T. E. Lawrence, 'Lawrence of Arabia', falls into both categories, and is a legendary figure in the Western imagination, romanticized every bit as much as the Arabs whom he himself romanticized. Other Western travellers whose accounts we explore are representative of the great numbers of people who visited the Orient, often with very little preparation for day-to-day living in a society very different to their own. Mr and Mrs Eden's adventures up the Nile without a dragoman are a source of unintentional humour. Dean A. Walker's summer jaunts in the 'Holy Land' prompted reflection on the average tourist's insulation from the people and realities of modern Palestine.

Dragomans themselves were engaged in activities far more complex than guiding and linguistic mediation. They were practitioners of what Mary Louise Pratt calls 'autoethnography', the act of interpreting particular images of one's own ethnic group to European travellers, including the images Europeans expect of them (Pratt 2008: 9). Dragomans were playing a part of which they were very aware: as dragomans, and as Orientals. When Thomas Cook and Sons exhibited at the St. Louis World's Fair in 1904, their displays on Palestine and Egypt were complemented by the participation of 'real' Palestinians and Egyptians. A photographic portrait of the dragoman Khalil S. Gandour of Jaffa, Palestine, appears on a contemporary postcard. An American visitor to the Fair records on it that he has 'spoken to this gentleman, his picture does not do him justice, he is fine looking and pleasant to talk to. He wrote his name on the card for me' (Figure 1). Gandour is presented as an agent and participant, not merely as a silent curiosity. At the World's Fair, he also met some former clients: members of the Cadbury family – the famous cocoa and chocolate company – whom he had twice guided in the Holy Land (Alexander 1906: 413). They drank Turkish coffee together and he showed them round the exhibition (Alexander 1920: 97). In published accounts of their travels, however, the tourists whom Gandour guided seldom mentioned him by name, and, if they did, this was merely in passing (Poe 1916: 88).

Dragomans often solicited letters of recommendation from their clients, and these started us on a paper trail towards reconstructing the personal

Figure 1: Postcard of Dragoman Khalil S. Gandour at the World's Fair, St. Louis, 1904. © Rachel Mairs.

and professional histories of dragomans, from their own perspectives. This book might have been called 'A Tale of Two Dragomans'. As we dug through archives, museum collections (and eBay), we discovered a wealth of contemporary documentary material on two individuals, whom we each pursued through published and unpublished papers: Daniel Z. Noorian (Muratov) and Solomon Negima (Mairs). Noorian, a young Armenian and an Ottoman subject, who spoke at least four languages, was employed as interpreter and overseer of workmen by two American expeditions that explored Babylonia and excavated the site of Nippur. He subsequently moved to the USA and established himself as a prominent antiquities dealer. Negima speaks to us, like many other dragomans, through the voices of his clients. From 1885 to 1933, he kept his testimonial letters, pasted into a leather-bound book, as a record of his career – for himself, and for potential future clients. Negima's pride in his work is clear in the care with which he has kept and collated positive feedback from foreign clients, some of them illustrious. In 2014, I (RM) bought this testimonial book on eBay, from a dealer in the United States. Did Negima, like Noorian, emigrate to the country whose citizens he had guided in his own?

The figure of interpreter is often a silent one – his voice either lost or overpowered by that of his employers. Perhaps the closest one can get to a dragoman's own perspective are the autobiographies of two men who worked as interpreters to the British officials and travellers in the first half of the nineteenth century. Although this time period falls beyond the scope of this book, the lives and careers of two adventurers, Giovanni Finati and Giovanni D'Athanasi, an Italian and a Greek, in some strange way echo those of Solomon Negima and Daniel Noorian, our main protagonists, and are worth mentioning here. Interestingly, both men knew each other and even worked side by side at the excavation of the Abu Simbel temple of Ramesses the Great (together with the infamous Giovanni Belzoni) (Finati 1830: II, 194–208).

Giovanni Finati (1786–1829?) left for posterity a hefty two-volume autobiography with an equally profuse title: *Narrative of the life and adventures of Giovanni Finati, native of Ferrara, who, under the assumed name of Mahomet, made the campaigns against the Wahabees for the recovery of Mecca and Medina; and since acted as interpreter to European travellers in some parts least visited of Asia and Africa.* The creation and publication of this book was ultimately made possible by William John Bankes (1786–1855), a well-known wealthy adventurer, explorer of Egypt and collector of Egyptian antiquities, and for some time Giovanni Finati's employer. Bankes encouraged him to dictate his book in Italian, and personally undertook the job of not only translating but also of editing and fact-checking, as well as adding occasional personal comments in footnotes. Quite fittingly, the book is dedicated to 'William John Bankes, Esq.' by 'his attached and faithful servant Hadjee Mahomet,' a name adopted by Finati at his conversion to Islam. Giovanni Finati's life was indeed worth telling. The eldest son of a family with small landed property, from Ferrara, he was studying to become a priest when northern Italy fell to Napoléon and, like many others, he was conscripted in 1805. He attempted to desert the army three times and finally managed to escape to Turkish Albania, converted to Islam and ended up in Egypt, a place he would call home from that moment on. He enlisted in the service of Mahomet Ali, the Pasha of Egypt, and participated in the expedition against the Wahabees under Tossoon Pasha, the favourite son of Ali. Having settled in Cairo, Giovanni found odd jobs as interpreter to several European travellers and eventually was introduced to William John Bankes, who offered him long-term employment on the trips to Upper Egypt and later to Jerusalem and Syria. Mr Bankes travelled in style; his retinue consisted of four people: one Portuguese servant, and three interpreters-attendants (including Giovanni) (Finati 1830: II, 72, 73, 74). Overall, Giovanni Finati seemed to have been a devoted attendant, interpreter and guard (he always travelled with pistols, see Finati 1830: II, 88) and was often referred to as Bankes' 'janissary' (Finati 1830: II, 109; D'Athanasi 1836a: 41, 45).

The Editor's Preface written by William John Bankes for Finati's autobiography, in addition to proclaiming the book to be of political and historical interest, might also be thought of as an advertisement of Giovanni's potential services as a guide and interpreter. He is described as an excellent companion and his 'truth and fidelity,' as well as surprisingly good memory, and the accuracy of his accounts, are emphasized (Finati 1830: I, vii–viii). In addition to these commendable personal qualities, what made him unique – at least in Bankes' view – was that 'he has been a traveller to no ordinary extent; and, possibly, that there is not any one living who has seen altogether so much' (Finati 1830: I, xix–xx). In addition, Giovanni Finati 'was personally acquainted with many of the most influential among the natives, and conversant with their language and habits' and his 'connexion also with the Egyptian army was no small point of recommendation' (Finati 1830: II, 53).

Having spent his youth in such a turbulent way, it was only natural that a quiet life did not agree with Finati. After a short stint of two years in Great Britain, Giovanni Finati (a.k.a. Mahomet) 'returned to seek fresh adventures in the East with Lord Prudhoe, who has engaged him during his travels as his interpreter' (Finati 1830: I, xxi) throughout 1826–9. This trip proved to be a success and his distinguished client, thoroughly satisfied with the services rendered by Finati, suggested that he should set up a permanent business as a guide and dragoman, not unlike that of Solomon Negima: 'it has been recommended to him to establish and superintend a small hotel for the accommodation of European passengers' (Finati 1930: I, xxiii). Unfortunately, this venture was never realized. The exact date of Giovanni Finati's death remains uncertain. As nothing is known about him after 1829, it is generally assumed that when his autobiography was being published in London he was no longer living.

Giovanni D'Athanasi (1798–1854), known to his employers and companions as 'Yanni', was born Demetrios Papandriopulos on the island of Lemnos. As his father had a small business in Cairo, 'Yanni' joined him there and went to school while studying the merchant trade for a few years. Having served briefly Colonel Ernest Missett, the Consul General of Great Britain, 'Yanni' was soon 'inherited' by Henry Salt, a new British Consul General, and by 1815 was his 'interpreter in Arabic and Turkish' (D'Athanasi 1836a: 3–4). Soon, his job was to encompass much more, and by 1817 'Yanni' was involved in excavating antiquities, still in the service of, and on behalf of, Henry Salt (Parkinson 2009: 77) – not unlike Daniel Noorian. Giovanni D'Athanasi resided in Thebes for at least eighteen years, in a house built by Salt, and, in addition to accommodating 'the English when they arrived there' (Madox 1834: I, 277; D'Athanasi 1836a: xix) and acting as their guide and interpreter, he soon became Salt's agent and was responsible for assembling the Consul's third collection of Egyptian antiquities (Taylor, Leach and Sharp 2011: 96). Eight years after Henry Salt's death in October 1827, Giovanni D'Athanasi travelled to London to participate and assist in the auction of the last collection of Salt, which was sold through Sotheby's in 1835 (D'Athanasi 1836a: 151). D'Athanasi's activity as Salt's agent and antiquarian was something that he intended to emphasize and use to advance his social standing as a dealer of antiquities in London. When his book entitled *A Brief Account of the Researches and Discoveries in Upper Egypt, Made Under the Direction of Henry Salt, Esq.* was published in 1836, in addition to his autobiographical account, which presented him as a capable interpreter, guide, and seasoned excavator, the book contained a catalogue of Henry Salt's collection of important Egyptian objects, already sold in 1835 (D'Athanasi 1836a: 153–261). It is perhaps not surprising that this publication coincided with the sale of another collection of Egyptian antiquities that D'Athanasi assembled for himself (Parkinson 2009: 222; Taylor, Leach and Sharp 2011: 97). This one was sold in London, also through Leigh Sotheby's, in 1836 (D'Athanasi 1836c). Prior to its sale, as part of the promotional campaign it had been exhibited at the Exeter Hall in the Strand, from November 1835 through January 1836, and a separate catalogue had been published (D'Athanasi 1836b). The exhibition of D'Athanasi's collection and its sale had been widely advertised in newspapers such as *The Times*, the *Champion* and the *Morning Chronicle*, to name just a few (Parkinson 2009: 222–4). Whatever remained unsold was offered at the follow up sale of a 'Very Magnificent and Extraordinary Collection of Egyptian Antiquities' which took place in 1837 (D'Athanasi 1837), and the 'residue' was sold through Sotheby's in 1845 (D'Athanasi 1845). Unfortunately, Giovanni D'Athanasi's career as antiquities dealer did not turn out to be nearly as successful as that of Daniel Noorian in New York. D'Athanasi decided to settle in London in 1849–50 and tried to establish himself as a dealer in pictures (Parkinson 2009: 225) but failed miserably. He died destitute in a boarding house in London in 1854 (Parkinson 2009: 225). For a Greek who spent most of his life in Egypt as a servant, attendant, interpreter and antiquities agent, his position in English society was 'ambiguous and marginal' despite his recently published autobiography and an attempt to emphasize his social connections with Henry Salt; and 'the man who had been a welcome contact for gentlemen in Egypt found that he was not considered a suitable acquaintance in London' (Parkinson 2009: 225 and note 11).

Giovanni Finati and Giovanni D'Athanasi, an Italian and a Greek, having found themselves in the East at an early age, and having adopted local languages and cultures, blended quite well into the flamboyant and variegated world of the Ottoman Empire. However, as interpreters and guides they remained forever trapped between the two worlds – convenient commodities to the travellers in the Orient, and bizarre misfits in the West.

Interpreting the Orient – in whatever guise it may appear in the Western imagination, as Arabia, Near East, Middle East – always involves the role of political power in the construction of knowledge. The act of interpretation, as we hope will become clear over the following chapters, is never one of transparent mediation. Across three generations of Edward Said's family, the Orient was interpreted to the Occident in dramatically different ways: by a dragoman to a German emperor; by a soldier in the US Army in the First World War; by a scholar whose analysis of the West's construction of the East has been translated from English into Arabic (Elmenfi 2013; Traboulsi 2009). The dragomans whose careers we consider here were agents, with the power to shape their clients' perceptions of the lands through which they travelled and the people with whom they came into contact. As contemporary accounts show, the figure of the dragoman himself also often became a kind of shorthand for the difficulties and frustrations which Western travellers experienced.

2

Mediating Language and Culture

Dragomans and Tourists

European and American travellers in the Orient looked for 'interpretation' on multiple levels: interpretation of sites and sights, often by reference to authoritative, printed works by Western scholars, interpretation of culture and, on a day-to-day practical level, interpretation of language. This chapter explores the people and tools (such as language instruction books) to which such travellers had recourse.

Visitors to Egypt and the Near East in the latter part of the nineteenth and early part of the twentieth centuries have left numerous, often seductively Orientalist, descriptions of their travels (Gregory 1999; a collection of excerpts may be found in Kalfatovic 1992). It is to these that we must turn for most of our evidence on the careers of contemporary interpreters. Their perspective is, inevitably, biased, and it must always be borne in mind that we are receiving a client-based perspective. These accounts might be viewed as the TripAdvisor of the period: their tendency is to report only very good or very bad experiences of dragomans, and otherwise to ignore them, on the assumption that their role as mediator is one of transparent communication.

There is a noticeable divide in travellers' accounts between those for whom the modern Middle East was an essential part of their experience – whatever their attitude towards this – and those for whom the modern Middle East was an annoyance, constantly tugging at their sleeves, capable of spoiling their enjoyment of an idealized Orient which owed more to the Western fantasy and control than to self-presentation. Travellers dreamed of a combination of the Land of the Pharaohs, the Land of the Bible and the Arabian Nights, and many interpreted what they saw and experienced so that they found what they wanted to find.

The motivations of many travellers were antiquarian. The sites and monuments of Egypt, Syria and Mesopotamia were a playground for those whose preoccupation with the ancient world ranged from the scholarly to the romantic. Photographic shots which juxtaposed the ancient and modern Orient were popular souvenirs (cover image). Nineteenth and early twentieth century Europeans and Americans of a socio-economic class able to afford foreign travel were likely to have had a Classical education, and we find in some accounts a prejudice about a changeless, intransigent Orient, which is supported by their reading of Herodotus' *Histories*. Western Christian travellers' interests and preconceptions were also heavily influenced by their knowledge of the Bible. Mesopotamia was the location of Old Testament cities such as Babylon, Nineveh, Erech and Ur of the Chaldees,[1] some of which were then in the process of being excavated. The decipherment of ancient Near Eastern scripts and languages, and the arrival of Near Eastern artefacts in museum collections in London, Paris and other capitals, increased still further the appeal of Mesopotamia as a travel destination. Egypt, too, held an important place in Judaeo-Christian scripture – quite apart from the intrinsic appeal of the civilization that had produced monuments such as the Pyramids and Sphinx. It had strong connections with the early history of the Jews and featured prominently in the narrative of the Books of Genesis and Exodus.[2] Egypt had also been a place of refuge for the Holy Family.[3]

This fascination with the ancient Near East attracted numerous travellers, scholars and package tourists, who indulged – according to their own tastes – in exploration, anthropology, survey, collection, excavation, plunder, theorizing and prophecy. Almost all such visitors, no matter how esoteric or academic their pursuits, however also had to deal with the modern Near East – with local people and conditions in general, and with the local authorities. Some of the travellers and archaeologists we will discuss in the following chapters learned to speak Arabic well. The majority of longer-term sojourners

---

[1] Babylon: Gen. 10.10; 11.9; Nineveh: Gen. 10.10–12; Jon. 3.3; 4.11; 2 Kgs 19.36; Isa. 37.37–8; Erech: Gen. 10.10; Ur: Gen. 11.28; 11.31; 15.7; Neh. 9.7.

[2] See, for example, Exod. 10; 12; Gen. 41; 47.

[3] Mt. 2.13–23.

in the East, however, especially at first, had to rely on interpreters, dragomans, translators and local guides – however they may have been termed. The role of interpreters is, and was, multi-faceted. Throughout history, bi- or multi-lingual individuals have often found themselves taking on (or being forced to take on) much more than just the task of interpreting. They have often played the roles of go-betweens, servants, bodyguards, pimps, diplomats, spies, messengers, managers and overseers, and have had to mediate, scheme and often improvise, be that in their official or unofficial capacity. They have also frequently been denied credit and recognition for their part in undertaking all these tasks, and have been vulnerable to discrimination or abuse (Mairs 2011).

The Profession of Dragoman

In Egypt the guide is called a dragoman. He puts on airs and has an inside pocket bulging with testimonials from people who were so glad to get out of his clutches that they willingly perjured themselves by giving him half-hearted certificates of good character. While you are in the hands of a dragoman you feel like a dumb, driven cow. You follow the fluttering night-shirt and the tall red fez of this arch villain for hours at a time, not knowing where you are going, or why. He takes absolute charge of you, either by making specious representa-tions or boldly assuming authority, and when you start out to visit the famous mosque of old Midullah Oblingahta or some other defunct celebrity you finish up in a junk shop for the sale of antiques, all of which are personally guaranteed by the dragoman, because he is a silent partner in the business. (Ade 1906: 165)

The American humorist George Ade wrote a comedic account of his travels in Egypt which will have resonated on a deeper level with most of the travellers discussed in the following chapters. The dragoman, or local interpreter and fixer, was an essential member of the retinue of European travellers in Egypt, a precedent set as far back as Herodotus in the fifth century BC (Figure 2). Many tourists had contemptuous attitudes towards their dragomans and their position, and many dragomans – whose testimony is more difficult to access – doubtless had trouble keeping their clients satisfied. Dragomans were inter-preters, mediators, guides and diplomats, and the title has the same semantic

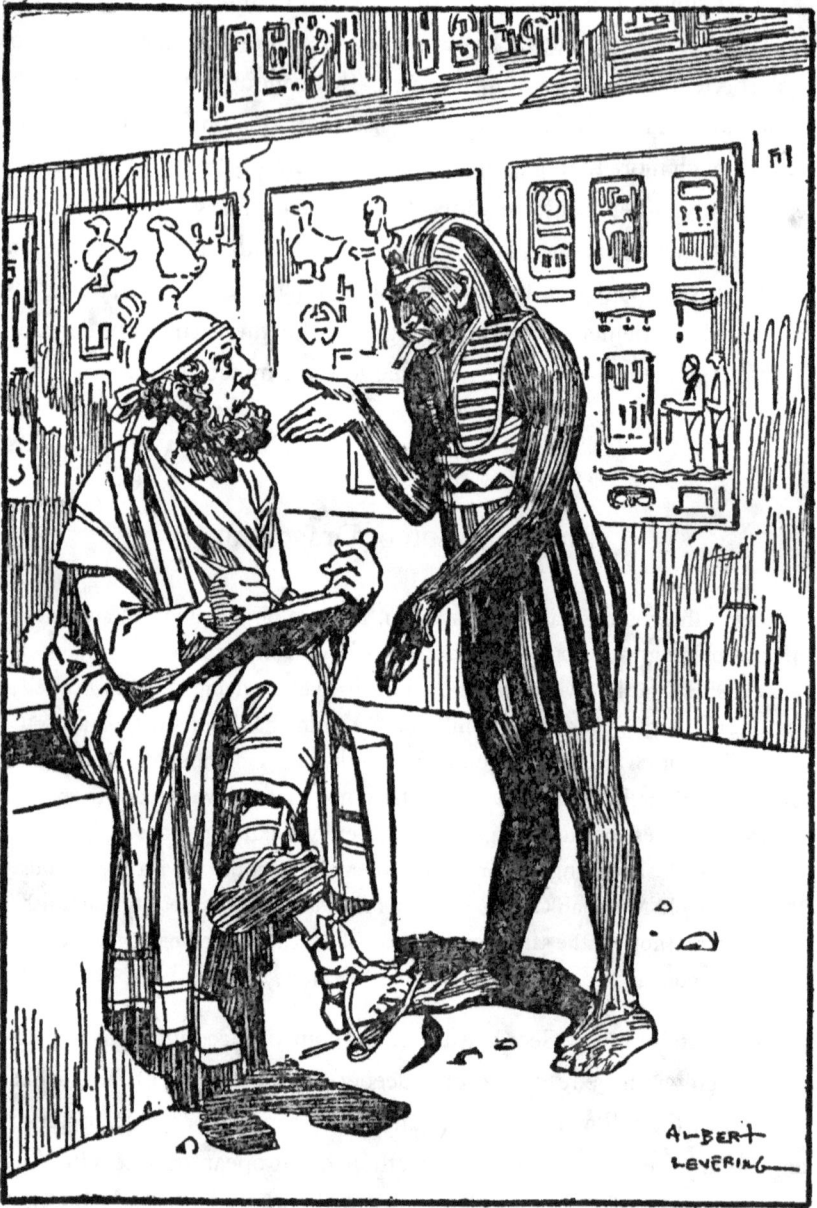

Herodotus put it all down—without batting an eye

Figure 2: Herodotus and his interpreter. From Ade 1906.

breadth as that of 'interpreter' in any number of other languages and historical contexts. The attitudes of some nineteenth century European and American tourists in Egypt to dragomans and the Arabic language are discussed here and are compared, in Chapter 3, to those of archaeologists and other longer-term sojourners in the country.

As we noted in Chapter 1, the role of the dragoman was, in part, to shield his client from the difficulties and inconveniences of travel in a foreign land and culture. Not all commentators viewed tourists' dependence on their dragomans in a positive light. Dean A. Walker, a Biblical scholar who went on to receive his PhD from the University of Chicago with a thesis on the negative verb in Semitic languages, thought that:

> the ordinary tourist is to be pitied. He sees the principal places when tired from a hard day's ride. He has not the language, and for information must depend on his 'Baedeker,' which is now on many points out of date, and on his dragoman, who thinks he is not earning his pound a day if his stories fall below the maximum size. He puts up at the best hotels, where English is spoken, and where everything else is English, and accordingly sees less of the life of the people. He may even, through his ignorance of the language, fall into disreputable habits that, if he be a minister, would shock his congregation at home. (Walker 1891: 97)

Many travellers, as we shall see, in fact embraced disreputable habits with great enthusiasm. Walker concedes that 'to travel with a dragoman is of course to escape most of these petty trials, but one has to pay for his exemption, and the cheating is done "in the lump" instead of at retail' (Walker 1891: 99).

For the average tourist, tackling 'The Nile without a Dragoman' – the title of an 1871 travelogue by Frederic Eden – was neither practical nor desirable. The Edens were on a tight budget, and could not afford a dragoman, although they acknowledged that these 'couriers of the East … smooth all difficulties, and stand between the traveller and nearly all annoyances' (Eden 1871: 4). They learned a little Arabic along the way, insufficient for all but the most basic purposes. They communicated in pidgin Italian with one of their servants, Ibrahim, and otherwise got by as best they could on gestures and the 'language' of baksheesh (a 'tip'; Eden 1871: 46). Upon their arrival in Alexandria, the Edens, in the way of the enduring stereotype of the Anglophone abroad, were frustrated at not being able to get by in English. Their local servants, politely but aggravatingly, pretended to understand what was said to them and tried their very best to appear obliging (Eden 1871: 9). What their Egyptian companions thought of these comic, incomprehensible foreigners is, of course, not recorded. *The Nile without a Dragoman* is dominated by accounts of penny-pinching and communication problems, with comparatively little in the way of historical or scenic commentary. One does not get the impression that sailing the Nile with the Edens can have been much fun.

For those with the money and inclination to hire a dragoman, the popular Baedeker guides had some advice, of a predictably Orientalist and pater- nalistic sort. In a section on 'Dealing with the Natives', it recommends that: 'Travellers about to make a tour of any length may avoid all the petty annoy- ances incident to direct dealings with the natives by placing themselves under the care of a DRAGOMAN'. First, the historical context is established:

> The word *dragoman* is derived from the Chaldæan *targem*, 'to explain', or from *targûm*, 'explanation'. The Arabic *targam* also signifies 'to interpret'. The dragoman was therefore originally merely a guide who explained or interpreted. Since the 7th cent. B.C. when Psammetichus I. threw open the country to foreign trade, against which it had previously been jealously closed, this class, which is mentioned by Herodotus as a distinct caste, has existed in Egypt. That author informs us that Psammetichus caused a number of Egyptian children to be educated by the Greeks in order that they might learn their language; and it was these children who afterwards became the founders of the dragoman caste. The great historian himself employed a dragoman, from whom he frequently derived erroneous information. A dragoman, who was employed by the governor Ælius Gallus to accompany him up the Nile, is accused by Strabo of absurdity, conceit, and ignorance. The ignorant Arabian, Nubian, or Maltese dragomans of the present day do not attempt to explain to translate the ancient inscriptions. An effort was recently made with some success to educate young Arabs for this calling in a school founded for the purpose; but, like most Oriental undertakings, the scheme has not been persevered with. (Baedeker 1878: 13)

There follows a description of the tasks a dragoman may be expected to perform, and some further words of wisdom on dealing with dragomans in one's service.

Similar descriptions and instructions appear in the Baedeker guides to Egypt, Palestine and Syria. Dragomans, the reader learns, can be expected to be fluent in one or more European languages (Baedeker 1876: 15, 21). They are more than 'mere interpreters', but they have their limitations:

> they are contractors for the management of tours and of caravans, and they relieve the traveller of all the difficulties of preparation and of intercourse with the natives. Throughout the whole journey they are useful in many important particulars; but in knowledge of the country, and especially of its antiquities, they are often sadly deficient. Dragomans in Syria are more than mere interpreters; So accustomed are they, moreover, like the horses and their owners, to certain beaten tracks, that it is often a matter of great difficulty to induce them to make the slightest deviation from the usual routes, which in all probability have been followed by the caravans for many centuries. (Baedeker 1876: 15)

As for choosing a dragoman, guidebooks published by specialists such as Baedeker and Murray provided lists of recommended individuals for cities such as Cairo, Jerusalem, Jaffa and Beirut. Such recommendations, the traveller was assured, were necessary because the majority of the profession were not to be trusted: 'There are about 90 dragomans in Cairo, all more or less intelligent and able, but scarcely a half of the number are trustworthy' (Baedeker 1892: xx; Figure 3: A Trusty Dragoman). The traveller was further advised to draw up a contract with his or her dragoman, spelling out itinerary and costs, templates for which were supplied in the guidebooks (Baedeker 1876: 16–17; Baedeker 1878: 460–1; Baedeker 1892: xx–xxi). Even with such a contract in place, 'even the best dragomans are inclined to patronize their clients, a tendency which must at once be quashed' (Baedeker 1892: xx).

The question of money crops up time and again in the guidebooks. The relationship between the traveller and local people is presented as a primarily economic one (Figure 4: The Dragoman who saw the Joke). Dragomans take their cut in dealings with shopkeepers. The language of baksheesh speaks loudest:

> The traveller, apart from his ignorance of the language, will find it exceedingly difficult to deal with the class of people with whom he chiefly comes in contact. The extravagance of their demands is boundless, and they appear to think that Europeans are absolutely ignorant of the value of money. Every attempt at extortion should be firmly resisted, as compliance only makes the applicants for bakhshish doubly clamorous. ... Thanks, it need hardly be said must never be expected from such recipients. ... The Egyptians, it must be remembered,

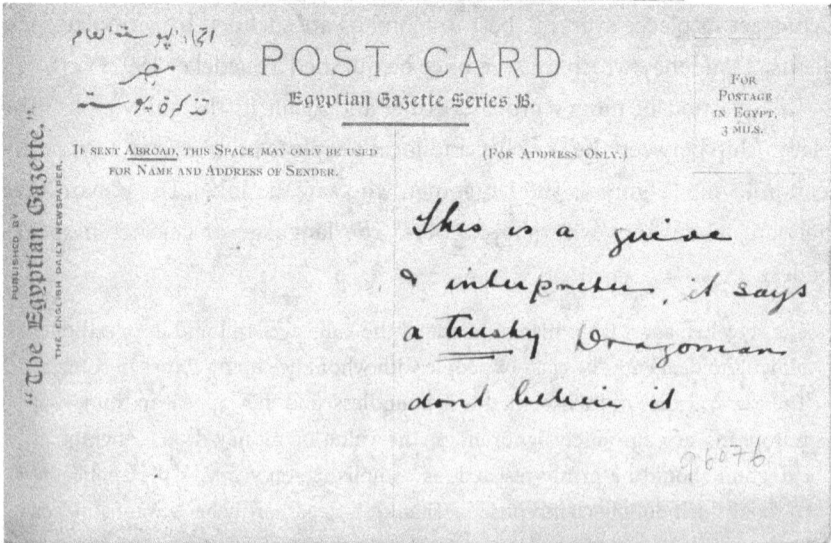

Figure 3: 'A Trusty Dragoman'. Vintage postcard, c. 1917. © Rachel Mairs.

PUNCH SUMMER NUMBER FOR 1937   June 7 1937

THE DRAGOMAN WHO SAW THE JOKE.

"BUT WE WERE TOLD THAT THE COST OF THIS TRIP INCLUDED TIPS."

Figure 4: 'The Dragoman who saw the Joke'. Punch, June 1937.

occupy a much lower grade in the scale of civilisation than most of the Western
nations, and cupidity is one of their chief failings; but if the traveller makes
due allowance for their shortcomings, and treats the natives with consistent
firmness, he will find that they are by no means destitute of fidelity, honesty, and
kindliness. Notwithstanding all the suggestions we have ventured to offer, the
traveller will to some extent have to buy his experience. (Baedeker 1876: 12–13.)

Even before they left home, from reading guidebooks and travelogues,
travellers will therefore have formed some impression of dragomans. They
might even have read newspaper stories such as 'Tyranny of the Dragoman',
a piece carried in *The Church Weekly* in November 1898. The dragoman, the

reader is informed, 'glories in the joy of having a white man under his thumb, and asserts his power in a hundred ways'. His command of many languages is put down to 'accident and low associations' (Hands 1898). Some travellers, as we shall see in the rest of this chapter, found the reality very different to that described in their Baedeker or Murray. Others found their prejudices confirmed.

The dragoman's side of the story is, of course, more complex. Dragomans found their way into the profession in different ways. The American jurist George Sherman Batcheller, who lived and worked in Cairo for a period in the 1870s–1880s, recalled how he once intervened with his English client on behalf of a donkey-boy, since which time:

> I have seen him grow to become a prosperous dragoman, who has served many an American family on the Nile. He has now retired with a competency, and there is no more respected citizen, no matter of what religious faith, in the city of Cairo. This is one of many similar incidents which have fallen within my observation. (Batcheller 1907: 773)

The role of dragoman was one of many in the tourist trade, and individuals might work their way up from managing animals to managing clients. Languages could be learnt on the job, or through primary education at a foreign-run school. The dragoman Solomon N. Negima, for example, whom we shall meet in Chapter 6, was educated at a German mission school in Jerusalem.

In the 1890s, there was a move towards creating a system of official certification for dragomans in Jerusalem, but this never really took off. A correspondent wrote in the Palestine Exploration Fund Quarterly Statement for 1893:

> One drawback when travelling through Palestine and Syria is the imperfect and unreliable information which is obtained through the ordinary Dragoman. He is helpful in many respects, but whether he has seen a copy of the 21 sheets of the Old and New Testament map of the Palestine Exploration Fund or ever read a number of the Quarterly Statement is doubtful. (PEFQ 1893: 2)

The dragoman was expected to interpret his country to outsiders in the language of contemporary European scholarship, and with an awareness of recent archaeological discoveries. The correspondent continues that the

Palestine Exploration Fund intended to run a series of lectures in Jerusalem, 'which series Dragomans are particularly invited to attend, and to take notes, and ask questions'. The municipal authorities next took up the campaign of educating dragomans:

> all Jerusalem dragomans are now required by the municipal government to pass an examination as to what they are to tell visitors to the holy places. The examiners are said to be the effendis of the mejlis – i.e., the magistrates of the bench – and those who pass successfully are to receive a diploma! (PEFQ 1895: 298)

Few such diplomas were to hang on the walls of the dragomans of Jerusalem. The American psychic, Ada Goodrich Freer, who lived in Jerusalem from 1901, reported that the scheme had achieved little in terms of improving the accuracy of guides' reports, but that gullible tourists got what they deserved (Goodrich Freer 1904: 217). Most travellers who hired a dragoman looked upon previous service to Westerners as the best form of qualification, demon-strated through signed letters of recommendation (Robinson 1901a: 329). A collection of such testimonials will be discussed in Chapter 6.

Innocents Abroad

Oriental travel in the second half of the nineteenth century had already descended into cliché. Numerous visitors to Egypt and the Holy Land published accounts of their travels, and many document at some length their experiences – positive and negative – with the dragomans in their hire. Well-known contemporary writers, such as Mark Twain, sent up these 'innocents abroad' (Twain 1869), and their naïve delight in even the most banal experiences. W. M. Thackeray, writing in 1846, found the travel journal a genre already ripe for satire. His *Cornhill to Grand Cairo* captures the beginning of mass tourism: an organized steamer excursion from England to Egypt. Edward Said thought the book 'moderately amusing' (Said 1978: 195), but at least one cannot doubt that Thackeray was having a good deal of fun on his Oriental jaunt. The same cannot be said for all the travellers whose accounts we will explore.

Already, in 1846, we find many of the clichés of Oriental travel which were to become standard in travel books, cut with a dash of knowing self-satire. Thackeray found it 'rather a fine thing to have a dragoman in one's service' (Thackeray 1846: 58), and gives several vignettes of dragomans and their clients interacting in stereotypical scenes. At Smyrna, he describes 'the young guide whom we hired to show us through the town, and to let us be cheated in the purchase of gilt scarfs and handkerchiefs, which strangers think proper to buy' (Thackeray 1846: 86). The tourists are routinely cheated by their dragoman: 'Our guide, an accomplished swindler, demanded two dollars as the fee for entering the mosque, which others of our party subsequently saw for sixpence' (Thackeray 1846: 50). The culmination of the trip is a visit to the pyramids:

> It was nothing but joking and laughter, bullying of guides, shouting for inter-preters, quarrelling about sixpences. We were acting a farce, with the Pyramids for the scene. There they rose up enormous under our eyes, and the most absurd trivial things were going on under their shadow. (Thackeray 1846: 152)

Thackeray, at least, was knowing. *Four Months in a Dahabëeh: Or, Narrative of a Winter's Cruise on the Nile* (1863), by M. L. M. Carey, was utterly sincere, and invited satire. The *Spectator*'s reviewer had evidently had quite enough of the genre, and did not mince his words:

> This is just one of those books which ought to exist, but in manuscript only. To all who know the authoress and her friends it has, we doubt not, a faint interest, like that of an old letter, and it may save herself the trouble of interminable descriptions, but it has no attraction for the general public. It is a mere young lady's journal of an uneventful Nile voyage, trite in subject, and unredeemed by any novelty of view or power in the descriptions. Egypt, as the seat of the oldest and most exceptional of civilizations, a land covered with relics of a past-away power and magnificence, the only morsel of Africa which has been the scene of visible progress, will always retain a high interest for the antiquary or the student. But Egypt as a place for descriptions of travel is almost exhausted; the Nile entirely so. The river is as familiar as the Thames, and the traveller, unless he has something new to say, or a just confidence in his power of working up old material, might as well publish an itinerary of his journey from Calais to Rome, and expect to interest the world in that new development of human energy. Miss Carey cannot boast of either qualification. ... We do not contest the right of an English lady to prefer to be ignorant if she pleases, but an authoress who

never saw the Koran, whose idea of describing antiquities is to say that they
may be made out with the assistance of Murray, and who has no capacity for
description, should not publish 400 big pages about Mohammedans and the
Nile. (*The Spectator*, 8 June 1863: 18)

If one is not looking for a serious disquisition on history or religion, Miss
Carey's book in fact has a certain charm. She had a jolly good time on the Nile
(not all tourists did), and her account is full of interactions with people as well
as monuments. She offers an excellent insight into the practicalities of a Nile
trip for the well-off Victorian traveller who was looking for an adventure, but
not too much of an adventure. Miss Carey was typical of many of the travellers
whose writings are discussed in this chapter, in that her intended audience
was made up of friends, family and other people of a similar background, who
might themselves have travelled to Egypt, or have wished to do so in the future:

> I can honestly state for the benefit of future adventurers, that we spent five
> whole months in Egypt, and that we enjoyed ourselves. It would make but a
> sorry home, it is true, but Egypt is well worth a visit; and because the friends
> in my truly favoured home would naturally expect something of me on my
> return, at the events of this 'warm winter' were carefully committed to paper,
> as they occurred; and now at the request of the same ends, I lay them before
> them, that they may be amused or stupefied over their pages as the case may
> be. (Carey 1863: 3)

Miss Carey's dragoman, Mohamed (whose name is seldom mentioned),
is a constant companion and source of assistance and information, whose
company she seems to have enjoyed and whose guidance she trusted. Trust or
its absence is a recurring theme in tourists' accounts of their dragomans. She
knew of the reputation of dragomans among travellers, but her own attitude
was relaxed, even passive, and she was content to be guided:

> We had only very slight experience of the trouble which these strange individuals
> sometimes give. Their knowledge of English raises them above their fellow-
> countrymen, and they consider themselves quite on a par with their masters, if
> not above them. (Carey 1863: 238)

She wished, on at least one occasion, that she could talk to local people in their
own language (Carey 1863: 146), but she seems to have been comfortable with
the level of insulation from the Orient which her dragoman provided. Things

which would have annoyed more independent travellers did not bother her particularly – such as the way in which her dragoman took charge of her souvenir shopping, at Luxor and Cairo:

> Our luncheon was spread in view of the beautiful columns of the Memnonium and the Catacombs in the hills, and a small bazaar of 'antiques' was gradually formed by the Arabs, who pressed round offering their goods for sale. A strange collection, and strange-looking merchants, with their dark faces and grinning white teeth. The dragoman and the guide discerning between what was truly ancient and what was only modern imitation, bargained and purchased for us, and as we knew nothing about the matter, we took all on trust from them, and set down each article as a treasure. (Carey 1863: 137)

> We discovered, towards the end of our visit, that the merchant in the Syrian bazaar understood English perfectly, but he feigned entire ignorance of the language in order not to hamper our intercourse with the dragoman on the subject of his wares. Mohamed also was perfectly aware of this fact, but he did not let it out, and continued to bargain for us, prefacing each fresh proposal with a washing of his hands, whereby he declared himself incapable of taking any of the extra prices for himself, as he loudly asserted that 'all other dragomans' did. We had good reason to believe that both merchant and dragoman were well up on their own interests on this occasion; yet, from future considerations, and comparisons with other travellers and their bargains, we found that these fatiguing hours in the bazaar had not been ill spent. The articles Mohamed el Adlëéh procured for us were of the best materials, and not too highly priced, as times go; indeed, we should not hesitate to apply to him for future bargains. (Carey 1863: 377–8)

Not all tourists were alike. We tend to hear of dragomans most often in contemporary accounts when clients resented their presence or 'interference'. But it is worth bearing in mind that many travellers, such as Miss Carey, were perfectly happy to be led by their dragomans, considering it part of the experience of Oriental travel. This did not make them dupes. Miss Carey rather enjoyed the way in which 'the histories of Moses, Joseph, and all the Egyptian pharaohs, were so jumbled together in the dragoman's brains, that there was no making head or tail of them, and they were intermingled with the most ridiculous traditions' (Carey 1863: 289–90). She shrewdly observed how Mohamed had been watching the group dynamics, and the subtle power and pressure the opinions of the ladies of the party put on their ostensible leader 'Cousin Phil', and had modified his own behaviour accordingly (Carey 1863: 238). This apparently submissive tourist is in fact asserting dominance over the pushy dragoman, by making him a character in her own fantasy of Oriental travel.

One of the most interesting aspects of the travellers' accounts which we explore in these pages is the development of the interpreter or dragoman as a stock character – often rascally – who does not always mediate his language and culture in a way which is satisfactory to his employer. Travel writing is a literary genre with its own tropes and conventions. In travelogues of the late nineteenth and early twentieth centuries, the dragoman is often cast as part of an Oriental scene, observed, described and judged by the European or American writer: "picturesqueness" ... was an absolute requirement; it was essential for the actors to look the part' (Gregory 1999: 130). Even those who had more practical, professional interests in the contemporary East lapsed into Orientalist fantasy. Charlotte Ehrlicher, an American nurse who visited local hospitals in Palestine, wrote of her 'dragoman with a gorgeous gown and turban' (Ehrlicher 1912: 430). An embroiderer (known only by the initials 'M.G.H.') combined description of the technical aspects of local needlework with a romantic story about a dragoman's family heirloom:

> The Orientals have a fine gold thread which they can draw through stuffs, as we have seen in their finely wrought towels and doilies. But I have found it very expensive. Moreover, we have no needle. A dragoman once gave to a friend of mine the family needle. It was two hundred years old, a dearly prized heirloom. It was three-sided, like a sail needle, although very fine. The thread passed through the apex of the triangle and came out the fiat side, which shielded it from cutting the cloth. In this way a path was made for the gold thread. (M. G. H. 1888: 123)

Occasionally, we can see the dragoman playing up to the image the traveller wishes to see of him. The American artist Georgia Timken Fry strays into purple prose:

> Those only who have had the privilege of spending a winter in Egypt, land of mystery and solemnity, can thoroughly appreciate a truthful representation of that fascinating country and understand why people who have been there are ever after haunted by a desire to return. Was it because on the last day of our stay, as, on all fours, we drank of the waters of the Nile, the Arab dragoman

said: 'Allah be praised! Master drinked from de Nile; he come back, sure!' (Fry 1918: 368)

Here we find the figure of the submissive, simple Oriental, depicted by a foreigner who is probably being laughed at behind her back.

From the accounts of many travel writers, it would seem that being cheated by one's dragoman (or feeling that one had been) was part of the experience of a journey in the East. Some even take a certain pleasure in being able to recount how they were ripped off – whether or not this was for any substantial amount. Gustave Flaubert's lively (and often racy) letters to family and friends in France contain descriptions of several dragomans. In general his view was that 'most dragomans are appalling scoundrels', but he was pleased to have found an exception in his own dragoman, Joseph, dismissive though he might be of the latter's capabilities and personal qualities:

> The [dragoman] is a gentleman who hasn't doffed his clothes a single time since we have had him; he is always dressed in toile and always saying '*Il fa trop chaud* [sic].' His language is incredible and his appearance even more curious. However, he is a hearty and worthy kind of fellow, with whom one could go to the Antipodes without a scratch. (Steegmuller 1972: 91–2, Letter to his mother, 18 January 1850, 3 February 1850)

Madame Flaubert received one version; her son had more explicit things to say in letters to other correspondents. One dragoman is 'one of the most arrant pimps, ruffians and old bardashes that could ever be imagined' (Steegmuller 1972: 41, Letter to Louis Bouilhet, 1 December 1849). In his extensive documentation of his erotic experiences in Egypt, he describes the peculiarities of 'love-making by interpreter'. Like many other travellers of his period, Flaubert picked up a little Arabic, but was essentially utterly dependent on his dragoman. Most Europeans could not converse with local Egyptians, and this meant that their experience of Egypt was one 'of reading or looking rather than listening ... [they] had little choice but to read the landscape because they could not speak the language' (Gregory 1995: 50–1).

Dragomans already depicted as part of an exotic, oriental scene, as we have already discussed, are furthermore set among a cast of colourful and covetous natives. Charles Dudley Warner, a friend of Mark Twain, wrote *My Winter on the Nile: Among the Mummies and Moslems* – a title which itself indicates the author's attitudes towards modern Egyptians as part of the same exotic landscape as the remains of their ancient predecessors. Warner describes himself as constantly importuned by local hangers-on:

> before we know it we are in a carriage, and a rascally guide and interpreter – Heaven knows how he fastened himself upon us in the last five minutes – is on the box and apparently owns us? (It took us half a day and liberal backsheesh to get rid of the evil-eyed fellow.) (Warner 1876: 32)

Like many other travellers, Warner is a believer in the communicating power of the language of baksheesh. He is also forthright in his judgements about the words of Arabic likely to be of most use. These include 'yes', 'no', shopping phrases, but, in addition:

> there are two other words necessary to be mastered before the traveller can say he knows Arabic. To the constant call for 'backsheesh' and the obstructing rabble of beggars and children, you must be able to say *mafeesh* ('nothing'), and *im-shee* ('get away', 'clear out', 'scat'). It is my experience that this *im-shee* is the most necessary word in Egypt. (Warner 1876: 305)

Here and there, however, *My Winter on the Nile* offers some perspective on the interpreting process itself: the agency exercised by dragomans and their approaches to their professional tasks. Warner observes that 'the dragomans never interpret anything, except by short cuts' (Warner 1876: 63), and that he is frequently given a briefer summary of the longer Arabic speech which he has heard. Amid his impatience and racism, Warner has moments of insight:

> The Eastern dragoman is not averse to talking, but he always interprets in a sort of short-hand that is fatal to conversation. I think the dragomans at such interviews usually translate you into what they think you ought to say, and give you such a reply as they think will be good for you. (Warner 1876: 108)

Managing Clients

To explain the attitudes of travellers and archaeologists to their guides and interpreters, we must first look at their expectations. What constituted a 'good' dragoman? Time and again, we find the concept of honesty held up as an ideal for dragomans. What this 'honesty' often equates to, in the eyes of the traveller, is total deference to the client's whims, and consistent action in his interests. A good dragoman also needed to be a cultural as well as linguistic mediator. He needed to act as a source of commentary on scenes which a traveller could see but not interpret. Ideally, he could 'draw a picture coloured by Western bias for Western consumption' (El Kholy 2001: 263).

What qualities did a dragoman think made him a good dragoman? A passage in Herodotus' *Histories*, written in the fifth century BC, resonated with many later travellers to Egypt:

> There is a notice in Egyptian script on the pyramid about how much was spent on radishes, onions, and garlic for the labourers, and if my memory serves me well, the translator reading the notice to me said that the total cost was sixteen hundred talents of silver. (Herodotus II. 125 [trans. Waterfield 1998])

The Greek word *hermēneus* can be used to mean a mediator in a number of senses, not merely a linguistic translator. The *hermēneus* could therefore be understood by Classically-educated nineteenth century travellers as a dragoman of sorts. The 1878 Baedeker guide to Egypt pointed out that Herodotus had probably been misled:

> It is unlikely that the interpreters, who attended travellers like the dragomans of the present day, were able to read hieroglyphics. They probably repeated mere popular traditions regarding the pyramids and other monuments, with embellishments and exaggerations of their own. (Baedeker 1878: 331)

The American humorist George Ade believed that Herodotus had been had:

> The breed [of dragoman] has not changed since 500 B.C. ... Herodotus discovered some large hieroglyphics on the face of the Pyramid and asked the guide for a translation. It is now supposed that the guide could not read. Anyone with education or social standing wouldn't have been a guide, even in that remote period. But this guide wanted to appear to be earning his salary and be justified in demanding a tip, so he said that the inscription told how much garlic and onions the labourers had consumed while at work on the job, and just how much these had cost. Herodotus put it all down in his notebook without batting an eye. (Ade 1906: 170–2)

Dragomans had to deal with a wide range of expectations, some of them unreasonable, from their clients. Matters of itinerary, food, accommodation and other everyday practicalities would be covered in a contract of the type the guidebooks recommended. Travellers could also turn out to expect unrealistic things. Many a guide probably ended up pretending to know hiero-glyphs in order to keep his clients happy, although we should not assume that all did not (Figure 5: Dragoman explaining cartouches):

> I knew an old lady who took a dragoman up the Nile and would never fail to ask him the meaning of each succeeding frieze of Egyptian hieroglyphics. Hassan, who could not read his native Arabic, let alone English, still less ancient Egyptian, would scan the surface gravely and reply: 'That, Miladi, mean "God very nice"', with which she was on each occasion perfectly satisfied. (Storrs 1937: 22)

Some travellers who knew that their dragoman was giving them inaccurate information did not mind: whether he was showing them the place where the angels appeared to the shepherds (Parker 1896: 351), or identifying birds on the Nile (Sherman 1915: 377), the dragoman's untruths were motivated by a desire to please, or by simple ignorance. Other travellers took misinformation as outright lies. The dragoman's motives were not always taken into account.

Security was another area in which clients' expectations came into conflict with dragomans' professional practice and local knowledge. The American

DRAGOMAN EXPLAINING CARTOUCHES IN THE TEMPLE OF KOMOMBO.
Mohammed, the chief Dragoman of Thomas Cook & Son in Egypt.

Figure 5: 'Dragoman explaining cartouches in the temple of Komombo' from Sladen 1911.

Biblical scholar George L. Robinson was determined to visit Kadesh and Petra, whatever local circumstances:

> Our dragoman's name was Hanna Abu Sa'ab, which, being interpreted, means 'John the Father of Difficulty.' This looked a little ominous. But again and again in our bargaining with him we stipulated that, no matter what obstacles might arise, or what detours might be necessary to reach our goal, we must at all hazards see 'Ain Kadis. Hanna had never been there before, and for our sakes it was fortunate that he had not, for very probably he would never have undertaken such a task a second time. I tried to get him to make a covenant of blood with us to the effect that he would show us Kadesh, but he refused. The contract between us, however, was formally drawn up and signed before starting, and sealed with the official stamp of the American consul in Cairo. And well was this precaution taken; for, four days before reaching 'Ain Kadis, Hanna and the servants formally endeavored to divert us from our course. (Robinson 1901a: 330)

> It had been the writer's earnest wish for several years to visit Petra, the ancient capital of Edom. On arriving in Cairo, however, he sought in vain for a dragoman who was willing to venture thither from the south. In Jerusalem also no native guide had the courage necessary to make the attempt. (Robinson 1901b: 6)

Here, one might read between the lines. The client wanted to visit these sites, even if it was not safe to do so. The dragoman is blamed for his cowardice or deception, when his reasons for refusing to go to these places may have been perfectly reasonable, and based on his client's safety and comfort as well as his own.

The perspective of the dragoman is lacking in almost all of the accounts we survey. Occasional asides, speculating on his motivations, are more often than not humorous or derogatory in intent. The American tourist George Ade, however, combines the usual frustration with his guide's dishonesty with some moments of insight into what it was like to make one's living as a dragoman:

> On the morning of our departure from Luxor Mahmoud came around for his letter of recommendation. I had worked for an hour to write something evasive which would satisfy him and not perjure me too deeply. When he came to the hotel I gave him the following:—
>
> To Whom It May Concern:—The bearer, Mahmoud, has been our dragoman for four days and has attended us faithfully at all hours; also, he has shown us as many temples as we wished to see.

He looked at the paper blankly and said, 'I do not read English.' At that Mr. Peasley brightened up. He read the testimonial aloud to Mahmoud and declared that it was incomplete and unworthy of the subject matter. In ten minutes he completed the following and the dragoman took it away with him, highly pleased:—

To Whom It May Concern—Greeting:—The bearer, Mahmoud, is a dragoman of monumental mendacity and commercial Machiavellism. His simulated efforts to faithfully serve us and protect our interests have had an altogether negative effect. Anyone employing him will find him possessed of moral turpitude and a superlative consciousness of his own worth. His knowledge of Egyptian history is enormously inconsequential, while his English vocabulary is amazing in its variety of verbal catastrophes. We commend him to travellers desirous of studying the native characteristics of the most geological stratum of society.

'He has made a lot of trouble for us, and now we've got even by ruining him,' said Mr. Peasley.

It seemed a joke at the time, but later on, when we thought it over, we felt sorry for Mahmoud and wished we had not taken such a mean advantage of him. After all is said and done, a man must make a living.

On our way back to Cairo from Assouan we stopped over at Luxor. Mahmoud, by intuition or through telepathy, knew that we were coming and met us at the station. He was overjoyed to see us again.

'I showed your letter to a gentleman from the Kingdom of Ohio,' said he, 'and it procured for me one of the best jobs I ever had.' (Ade 1906: 287–9)

Mahmoud (or rather, the literary character of Mahmoud) is a lovable rogue, a trope which occurs time and again in travellers' accounts of their dragomans. But he is also an individual with his own personality and motivations.

Learning Arabic

Not all dragomans were flesh and blood. Some travellers aspired to guide themselves, and took printed books along as their 'dragomans' in engaging with the Arabic language and culture. The first place where travellers with a desire to communicate with local people might turn was to their trusty Baedeker or Cook's Handbook, but in fact they often had to go out of their way to find such guidance. The guidebooks issued by travel companies, such as Thomas Cook and Son's, or Shepheard's Hotel in Cairo, were not designed for the kind of independent travellers who wanted to make their own way in Arabic. Another way of looking at it is that tour operators actively discouraged language learning, encouraging reliance on their own services. *Cairo and Egypt: A Practical Handbook for Visitors to the Land of the Pharaohs* was presented to the guests of Shepheard's Hotel. It contained an Arabic-English vocabulary, but no grammar or separate list of phrases:

> Those who are desirous of acquiring a fuller knowledge of Arabic are recommended to use the small, practical grammar by Haggenmacher, Sosin and Vollers, or the larger one by Spitta, and the linguistic guide by Hartmann. In any case it is necessary to employ a native teacher. (Particulars at the Inquiry Office.) (Shepheard's 1895: 101)

Shepheard's, at least, were supportive of further study, albeit with teachers contracted through the hotel. Cook's Tourists' Handbooks for Egypt and for Palestine and Syria were less helpful. The 1876 Handbooks for these regions contained no information on the Arabic language at all (Thomas Cook 1876a; Thomas Cook 1876b), a practice followed in subsequent editions. The Handbooks recommended Cook's own system of pre-paid coupons, and tourists were warned against making their own, independent arrangements:

> The Travelling Coupons issued by THOS. COOK & SON are now so well known and universally used, that it is unnecessary here to enter into particulars about them. Suffice it to say that they have been found to be advantageous to all European travellers, and in the East, where travelling is under greater difficulties in every respect, their system is indispensable to those who are unable to grapple with the obstacles presented by not being acquainted with Oriental languages, and with having to deal with dragomans and others, whose demands are invariably exorbitant. (Thomas Cook 1876a: 8; Thomas Cook 1876b: 9; this text is repeated in subsequent editions, such as Budge 1897: 27–8)

In the early 1870s, Cook's were attacked in the British press by independent dragomans, who accused them of slander, and of unfair business practices (see Chapter 6). The tourist market in Egypt and Palestine at this period was competitive, and growing. It was not in Cook's interest to let potential clients think that they could learn sufficient Arabic to get by on their own. Many, of course, would not have been inclined to do so in any case, and found the system of coupons and pre-arranged dragomans convenient and to their liking. Just as in the present day, different people preferred different styles of travel.

Other guidebooks offered travellers greater assistance with Arabic, but even some of this was of questionable practical use. The first John Murray handbook for Egypt (Wilkinson 1847) led with the practicalities: a very lengthy English-Arabic vocabulary, including notes to the effect that it was in the colloquial dialect of Egypt, but with no section on grammar. It was published just before Flaubert's visit to Egypt, and it supplies much material which he might have found useful, such as affectionate Arabic addresses to a woman, presumably for use in recreational contexts rather than polite company: 'My dear to a woman. ya ḥabéebte, ya aýnee, ya aynáy, ya ayóonee, *i.e.* my eye, my two eyes; ya róhee, my soul' (Wilkinson 1847: 52). The 1858 Murray's Handbook for Syria and Palestine has a much briefer vocabulary, restricted to travel terminology and guidance on the pronunciation of place names, and a more sober tone: 'The Bible is the best handbook for Palestine; the present work is intended to be a companion to it' (Porter 1858: xi).

Just as in their businesslike instructions on hiring and working with dragomans, the guidebooks published by Baedeker provide more practical information on the Arabic language, and greater encouragement to persevere. The 1876 Baedeker for Palestine and Syria, and the 1878 version for Egypt, contain similar sections on the history of the Arabic language; its phonology and the importance of practising correct pronunciation (Baedeker 1876: 106: 'The numerous gutturals of Arabic render the language unpleasing to the ear'); and the alphabet (Baedeker 1878: 189: 'It is greatly to be wished that the Arabs would adopt a simpler alphabet, with a regular use of the vowel-signs, and that they would agree to write the ordinary spoken language. The present condition of affairs not only seriously increases a stranger's difficulties in learning the language, but is a serious obstacle to the education of the Arabs themselves'). There follows a list of words and phrases in the appropriate dialect, of Egypt or the Levant, in transliteration:

The above remarks are made merely in order to afford a slight idea of the structure of the language. the difficulties of which are such that few persons will venture to encounter them, unless they make a prolonged stay in the country. We should, however, recommend the traveller to commit to memory the following words and phrases of everyday occurrence, a knowledge of which will often prove useful. (Baedeker 1876: 107)

Short dialogues, 'On Arrival', 'At the Custom-House', 'At a Shop', give the learners some words and phrases in practical contexts. These include, of course, the phrase 'I do not speak Arabic', which to an Egyptian or Palestinian interlocutor must have been obvious enough.

How useful did travellers actually find these language guides? One American tourist in the early 1900s offers an insight:

> Mr. Peasley actually bought one of those 'Arabic at a Glance' books and started to learn some of the more useful sentences. He said that if he could get Arabic down pat he would pass as a native and be enabled to buy things at about half price. After two days of hard study he attempted a conversation with a military policeman standing on the river bank at Dendera. Mr. Peasley strolled up to him, careless like, and said, 'Ana awez arabiyet kwayesset min shan arookh el balad.' That was supposed to mean, 'I want a first-class carriage for driving in the town.' The stalwart soldier gazed at Mr. Peasley with a most bewildered look in his jet black eyes and then began to edge away.
>
> 'Hold on,' said Mr. Peasley. 'How about hal yel zamna ghafar yerafegua bill tareeg?'
>
> Mr. Peasley thought he was asking, 'Shall we require a guide or an escort in this town?'
>
> The soldier beckoned to us to come over and help him out.
>
> 'Tell him, please, that I am educate at the Presbyterian Mission,' said he. 'I speak only English and Arabic.' (Ade 1906: 210)

Ade, a humorist, is setting up a punchline, but the experience of unsuccessfully reading Arabic from a phrasebook, without practice or a trained ear for Arabic phonology, is likely to have been that of many tourists. On the page, Mr Peasley's Arabic is perfectly correct, but when he tries to use it an Egyptian mistakes it for Russian.

For those who were inclined to study Arabic more thoroughly, yet without committing themselves to full-time academic study, resources were available. The problem of not speaking the local language was keenly felt by many travellers, and some, at least, were eager to develop a good command of Arabic and to benefit from the increased independence this would give them:

Here, then, is one of the difficulties which immediately confront the Englishman, who is seldom a good linguist. For the full enjoyment of Cairo a little French and rather more than a smattering of Arabic are essential, and the latter, at any rate, is not easily acquired. Consequently the tourist is at the mercy of his dragoman for any information, and misses those snatches of 'chaff' and repartee among the natives which often add so much to the day's amusement. With commendable energy travellers frequently, and after much labour, learn a few Arabic phrases, usually *questions*, forgetting that they cannot possibly understand the replies. Let me recommend them to confine their earlier efforts to the acquisition of such sentences only as give absolute instructions to servants, drivers, etc., and to which no response is required. (Kelly 1902: 13)

Robert Talbot Kelly (1861–1934) was an artist who lived in Cairo from 1883 to 1915, constantly interacting with local people as he painted scenes of everyday Egyptian life. He learnt Arabic to a high standard, and his *Egypt Painted and Described* is the product of the freedom of movement, social experiences and local knowledge which this gave him. Kelly was only the latest in a long line of long-term European residents in Egypt who learnt the language fluently and got to know the country well – even if their reports of it are still marked by the perspectives, and often prejudices, of an outsider. Shorter-term residents or sojourners, following Kelly's advice, might still gain a good, basic knowledge of Arabic. In addition to practice with local teachers, there were books which they might use, at a level above that of the tourist guidebook but below that of a scholarly grammar of the Classical language – of which I review only a small selection here.

One of the best is Yacoub Nakhlah's *New Manual of English and Arabic Conversation*, published in Cairo by the Khedive's Press in 1874. Its approach to explaining Arabic grammar is practical, and focuses on rules and patterns which will 'render the students competent to speak the language and make himself clearly understood by all classes of Arabs' (Nakhlah 1874: Preface). The vocabulary and dialogues are laid out in three columns: English, Arabic in Roman script, Arabic in Arabic script. Nakhlah's intention is to make the work 'a practical hand-book of Arabic for the use of English and American travellers on the Nile; and a useful manual of conversation for the interest of natives desirous of acquiring the English language'. The great strength of the *New Manual* is its focus on conversation, common expressions and general small talk. It succeeds in communicating something of the way in which Arabic is actually spoken, in social contexts. (There is a remarkably extensive section on phrases to be used in playing a game of cards.) If I were a traveller on the Nile in the 1870s, and wanted to have interesting social interactions with local people, I would choose Nakhlah.

In the 1880s, as more Europeans and Americans travelled in Egypt and the Levant, other Arabic language guides came on the market. Some were designed specifically for the use of the British army in Egypt, with an appropriate array of phrases (Green 1883; an earlier example, for use in the Indian Civil Service, is Forbes 1868). One popular handbook was *Arabic Self-Taught*, by A. Hassam, which over the years was revised in several editions for different dialects of Arabic. The first edition, in 1883, was subtitled *The Dragoman for Travellers in Egypt* and billed as 'a new practical and easy method of learning the Arabic language'. Hassam begins with some encouraging words for learners:

> Eastern languages are not difficult to acquire, on the contrary, they are easily learnt, and any ordinary capacity can acquire a knowledge of them in a short time. ... A Traveller thus becomes his own Dragoman, and in using these simple Self-taught systems will not only add greatly to his knowledge, but enjoy his sojourn in the East with advantage and profit. (Hassam 1883: vi)

The 'Self-Taught' formula was a successful one, although it is difficult to glean any further information on just how many tourists were thereby enabled to become their own dragomans. Later editions of the book were marketed under the imprint of Franz Thimm's 'Self-Taught Library', based on a simple and practical method for Universal Self-Tuition in European and Oriental Languages', a series which was advertised in Cook's Handbooks. The 1898 edition of *Egyptian Self-Taught* was published without acknowledgement of Hassam's contribution, even though some sections were reproduced verbatim (Thimm 1898). Arabic script was removed, and words given only in Roman transliteration. The proofs were revised by Flinders Petrie, whose own experiences in learning Arabic will be explored in Chapter 3. His touch can be seen in the addition of phrases which would be of little use to the average traveller but indispensible to the archaeologist ('Are there mud bricks or burnt bricks?').

In 1915, the Reverend Naser Odeh produced a major revision of Hassam's original work, adapted to Syrian Arabic. Rev Odeh was T. E. Lawrence's first

Arabic teacher (see Chapter 3). Like its predecessors, this handbook was intended to be practical: 'The Vocabularies and Conversations have been carefully selected for practical use in the daily life of tourists, travellers, missionaries, business men, and all who come into contact with the natives of Syria' (Hassam and Odeh 1915: 3).

The *Arabic Self-Taught* books present the learner with vocabulary under separate category headings, and a grammar section, with exercises to be learned and copied out. Their format would appear familiar to many students of European languages, past and present. Some of Rev Odeh's additions, however, offer particular insights into the experience of an Anglophone traveller in Syria and Palestine, as well as the author's own viewpoint on good practice in language learning:

'I cannot learn Arabic if you speak English to me.'
mā aqdar at'allam 'arabi idha kunt tukallimni bil-inglīzi (103).

'He is entitled to ask two piastres, and is asking for baqshish, because it is hot
    and the luggage is heavy.'
ḥaqqu qirshain watālib bakhshīsh, lianid-dunya shaub wal'afsh thaqīl (112).

'Have you English beer?'
fī 'indak bīra inglizīyah? (118).

'We all enjoyed our excursion, only the ladies are a little tired.'
kulluna inbasaṭna fi safratna-l-qaṣira, faqaṭi-s-sittāt ta'bānāṭ shuwaiyah (124).

The words and phrases given in other contemporary language guides are similarly tailored to the needs and expectations of European travellers, whatever their native language. Once again, the dragoman appears as a metaphor for understanding and interpreting the East. *Le drogman arabe* is an excellent little study and reference book, published in Beirut by Joseph Harfouch (Harfouch 1894; Figure 6: Le drogman arabe). Like Hassam's *Arabic Self-Taught*, it went through several editions and evidently sold well. Harfouch was, in his own way, a dragoman. He wrote textbooks for French speakers to learn Arabic, and for Arabic-speakers to learn French. *Le drogman arabe* was intended for use in Syria, Palestine and Egypt, and Harfouch shows an awareness of his audience, their priorities and limitations:

Figure 6: Le drogman arabe.

Les étrangers, attirés dans notre pays par une large et cordiale hospitalité, n'ont pas ordinairement le temps d'étudier à fond la belle mais difficile langue arabe. (Harfouch 1894: v)

No Arabic script is used in the book, but there is a lengthy guide to grammar and syntax. Like Nakhlah with his focus on practical guidelines rather than comprehensive, formal grammatical rules, Harfouch does not drill the student in grammar for the sake of grammar. He supplies enough information, in an accessible manner, for the user to be able to construct his or her own sentences. Harfouch's audience, however, were very different from the kind of traveller who might pick up a teach-yourself book in preparation for a foreign holiday today. They were more likely to have been educated in their own language in a way that stressed formal grammatical structures, and to have learnt ancient and modern languages through the grammar translation method (for an overview of historical Euro-American language teaching methods, see Richards and Rodgers 2001: 3–17). Using this grammatical and syntactical grounding, the student could then move on to create his or her own dialogue using a list of useful words, presented under categories such as animals and plants, food and drink or commerce. Another similarity with Nakhlah's book of twenty years earlier is that Harfouch gives an unusually extensive list of forms of address and civilities, which gives greater scope for real interaction with Arabic-speakers than do many other phrasebooks.

Le drogman arabe does not neglect the practical needs of its users. Several pages are devoted to dialogues 'Avec un marchand de curiosités orien-tales,' and the reader learns to haggle in Arabic. If the traveller needs a 'real' dragoman, then there is another section entitled 'Pour engager un drogman', which supplies useful phrases:

'âyez tourjmân châter ya'ref frinsâwi, inglizi, 'almâni
Il me faudrait un bon drogman qui sache le français, l'anglais et l'allemand.

ana a'ref tourjmân yeḥki *ou* yatakallam inglizi ṭaïyb
Je connais un drogman qui parle bien l'anglais.

ent tourjmân
Vous êtes drogman?

ma'ak (wiyâk) chahâdât
Avez-vous des certificats?

warjini yâhom
Montrez-les-moi.

yebân ʿalaïk tourjmân ṭaïyb chahâdâtak kouwaïsé
Vous paraissez être un bon drogman car vos certificats sont excellents.
 (Harfouch 1894: 337–8)

It is interesting that a French guide to Arabic tells the reader how to arrange an
English- or German-speaking dragoman. Multilingual Europeans sometimes
had to be flexible in selecting from the dragomans available. I will return to
the question of a dragoman's certificates in Chapter 6, when we explore a
collection of real testimonial letters from a Syrian dragoman, Solomon N.
Negima.

 The metaphor of the dragoman proved to be an enduring one in Arabic
textbooks for speakers of European languages. In addition to the examples
already discussed, we find the *Arabischer Dragoman für Besucher des Heiligen
Landes* (Wolff 1857), *Le dragoman – vocabulaire du voyageur: français, anglais,
arabe / The Dragoman – Traveller's Vocabulary: English, French, Arabic* (Elias
1935?) and *The Dragoman in the Pocket* (Gayed [n.d.]). The metaphor was
also applied in Arabic. *Qalā ʾid al-jumān fī fawā ʾid al-tarjumān / Instructions
aux drogmans* was a trilingual vocabulary, aimed primarily at Arabic- and
Turkish-speaking students of French (Miṣrī 1850; Figure 7). In the first
decades of the twentieth century, however, the living dragoman was becoming
a less familiar companion to travellers. Phrasebooks and beginners' guides
to Arabic also show new priorities, as they kept abreast of developments in
society and technology.

 New handbooks now frequently justified their existence to their readership.
Although our focus in this book is on Egypt and the Levant, and primarily on
English-language materials, the publishing industry in French-controlled North
Africa also produced instructional materials for Arabic (Larzul and Messaoudi
2013 present a fascinating study of these materials). Brahim Fatah, Director
of the École Arabe-Française at Algiers, authored a *Méthode directe pour
l'enseignement de l'arabe parlé, rédigée conformément aux nouveaux programmes*,
the result of his long experience of teaching Arabic to Europeans (Fatah 1912,
second edition). The title page bears a legend which reads more elegantly
in the Arabic than in the French: ʿal-lisān yukammil al-insān – L'homme se

(۰۱۲۵۰)

DIALOGUE 6.ᵐᵉ SUR L'ÉTUDE DE LA LANGUE FRANÇAISE.	التنبيهكمكالمه فرانسز لسانى تحصيل ايتمك اوزره	المكالمة السادسة في تحصيل اللغة الفرنساويه

Apprenez-vous le français?	فرانسزجه اوقور ميسكز ــ فرنسزجه تك تحصيلنه چالشيور ميسز	هل تقرؤون اللغة الفرنساوية؟ ــ هل أنتم مشتغلون بتعليم اللسان الفرنساوى
Oui, monsieur.	اوت افندم	نعم باسيدى
Vous avez raison; c'ést une langue si universellement répandue qu'il est honteux de ne pas la savoir.	بك اصابت ايتشسكز زيرا بولغت اوقدر مشهور ومقبولدركه بلماسى عيب ما يلور ــ حقكز واردر زيرا لسان مذكور روى زمينده اوقدر شهرت وانتشار بولشدركه تحصيل ايتميى بادى مجبو بيدر	الحق معكم لان هذه اللغة صارت الآن مشهورة بين الأنام حتى ان عدم معرفتها بارى من العيب ــ انصفتم لان هذا اللسان قد انتشر غاية الانتشار بحيث ان عدم تعلمه يعد عيبا
On parle français dans tous les pays de l'Europe.	بتون اوروپاده فرنسزجه تكلم ايدرلر ــ فرنكستانك اولكه لرنده فرنسجه لا قردى ايدرلر	اللغة الفرنساوية يتكلم بها في سائر بلاد اوروبا ــ الآن الناس تتكلم بالفرنساوى في كل اقطار الافرنج
On parle français dans toutes les parties du monde.	ديانك بتون اقسامنده فرنسزجه سو يلرلر	يتكلم باللسان الفرنساوى في جميع اقطار الدنيا
D'ailleurs, la littérature française est si riche et si belle qu'elle offre une source intarissable de plaisir à celui qui est en état de l'apprécier.	اندن ما عدا فرنسز لك ادبياتى اوقدر ظريف ومتسعدركه من اياسنه مطلع اولان اصلا اوصانمز	وغير ذلك اديات الفرنسيس ظريفة وممتعة جدا بحيث من عرف من مزاياها ووقف على خفاياها لا يأسأ ما اصلا
On y lit l'histoire de toutes les nations, leurs progrès, leurs décadence leurs lois, leurs mœurs et leurs gouvernements.	سائر ملل ودول تاريخ لارينى وايدرولوب قوت بوله لها اقراض واجمعلا للرين وقوانين متنوعه لله اصول كو متاريخ واخلا قلرينى شامل كاپلروار در	يوجد في هذه اللغة مؤلفات لا تحصى مشتملة على تاريخ سائر الملل والدول وتقدمها وأعمالها وزوالها ومحتوية على قوانينها واخلاقها وحكمها

۰(۳۲)۰

Figure 7: An extract from Khalīfah ibn Maḥmūd al-Miṣrī's *Qalā'id al-jumān fī fawā'id al-tarjumān / Instructions aux drogmans* (1850).

perfectionne par la connaissance des langues'. The problem of dialect was increasingly recognized: there was a need for works tailored to the colloquial speech of different regions. Spoer and Haddad's *Manual of Palestinean Arabic for Self-Instruction* was designed to fill a gap in the market. There were plenty of manuals in English for Egyptian and Lebanese Arabic, but tourists using these would sometimes have difficulty making themselves understood in Palestine:

> I have sought to adapt this work to the Arabic student interested in the dialect as such, as well as to those requiring the language for daily use in Palestine; also to the passing traveller seeking to make himself understood, and to understand those about him. In these days of multiplication of railways, hotels, and other conveniences of travel, when the often obtrusive dragoman is happily becoming less of a necessity, the demand for a practical phrase-book is increasingly urgent. The necessary limits of such a Manual obviously preclude the possibility of presenting a Grammar which is exhaustive, even in regard to the vernacular; it is however hoped that it may be found to include all that is necessary for such practical use as has been suggested. (Spoer and Haddad 1909: iii)

The phrases for travellers were now mostly about trains, horses and hotels, with no section on hiring a dragoman.

The dragoman is also conspicuously absent from *Dirr's Colloquial Egyptian Arabic Grammar, for the use of Tourists*, although the term does appear in the vocabulary. The authors' words of encouragement for the learner, on the other hand, are familiar from many earlier textbooks:

> One should not allow oneself to be frightened by the tales of the excessive difficulty of learning Arabic; colloquial Arabic has very few stumbling-blocks. Russian and Hungarian are much harder; for my own part I maintain that French necessitates much more work. Even in the case of the notorious verb, the student will soon see that all its different forms have in reality but one conjugation. It really is not very difficult to initiate oneself into this vigorous language in a comparatively short time The student who has worked thoroughly through the grammar and the reading-matter will soon find his bearings in other books, especially in reading-books, and, if he has the good fortune to be able to put his knowledge to the practical test in the land of the Pharaohs, he will make rapid progress. (Dirr and Lyall 1904: iv)

Learning some Arabic made it possible for travellers to experience Egypt and the Holy Land in new ways, and with greater independence. Those who had developed a good command of the language, such as the artist Robert Talbot

Kelly – and, as we shall see in the following chapter, many archaeologists – tended to be encouraging of others' efforts and dismissive of the common notion that Arabic was too difficult to learn. Tour operators, understandably, promoted the view that Arabic was too great a challenge, and unnecessary for travellers who had good tour arrangements. There was a range of factors at play, and many tourists on trips of only a few weeks' duration will have found a basic vocabulary, perhaps restricted to essential greetings and requests, quite sufficient for their needs. Others will have found learning and using some Arabic to be a central part of their enjoyment of their trip.

Despite their differing approaches, the language guides discussed above have some features in common. They provide guidance on Arabic pronunciation, while cautioning that it is best to learn from a native speaker. Many of them explain to readers the importance of using the correct dialect for the region in which they are travelling. They distinguish between the classical or formal educated Arabic of conventional grammars and the colloquial language which travellers will actually encounter. They give, alongside their vocabularies, at least some appropriate social small talk, and some insight into the social and cultural aspects of language use. Some are better in this respect than others. The examples which I have considered reveal a flourishing language book publishing industry in Cairo, Jerusalem and Beirut, as well as in foreign cities such as London and Leipzig. The authors were almost always native speakers of Arabic who had been educated in French or English, and they state directly in their prefaces that their anticipated readership is made up of curious travellers, not of desk-bound scholars in Europe or America.

What of the users of such guides? We tend to hear only of the very successful or the utterly overwhelmed: the Robert Talbot Kellys and the Mr Peasleys. Many a self-instruction book probably sat unopened at the bottom of a trunk for an entire Nile voyage. Original copies of these books can sometimes be picked up from booksellers in remarkably good condition, suggesting that they were not toted around the streets of Jerusalem in the heat and dust, their pages constantly thumbed.[4] A living, professional dragoman will, for most travellers, have rendered his printed namesake unnecessary.

---

[4] My own copy of the 1883 edition of Hassam's *Arabic Self-Taught* bears an owner's inscription of 1885. It is absolutely pristine. RM.

In the following chapters, we turn to examining how some famous figures in the archaeology of Egypt and the Levant dealt with the Arabic language and with dragomans. Many became accomplished Arabic speakers, who learned through a combination of book study and prolonged immersion. In the field, archaeologists lived and worked with Arabic speakers. Their priorities were rather different from those of the average tourist: they needed words for archaeological tools and methods, and they needed to be able to interact with their colleagues, workers and officialdom. Some had also to adapt to different dialects as they moved from one region to another. Professional dragomans also enter the picture: archaeologists were glad to be able to dispense with them, but frequently encountered them in the service of visitors to their excavations, or as dealers in antiquities. The relationship between archaeologist and dragoman was seldom a warm one.

3

Archaeologists in the Field

Flinders Petrie in Egypt and Palestine

Sir William Matthew Flinders Petrie (1853–1942) was a pioneer of scientific archaeology, who excavated in Egypt and later in Palestine (Drower 1995). We have already encountered him, in Chapter 2, as a contributor to Thimm's *Egyptian Self-Taught* (1898), who offered his own thoughts on which Arabic would most be useful for someone new to the language and to Egypt.

As far as Petrie was concerned, a traveller who wished to make the most of his or her time in Egypt should learn some Arabic. In his account of his 1887 season in Egypt, Petrie describes the scene on arriving at Aswan, where the human geography comprised:

> the Maltese grog-shop, the Arab, the Nubian, and the wild desert Bedawin with their enormous heads of dressed hair, the officer who evidently thinks that the first duty of every human being is to learn English, the suave Italian dealer, ancient tablets of past ages standing mute witnesses on the granite rocks at every corner, and Tommy Atkins [the personification of the English soldier], his parades, his stores, and his bands pervading the whole place. (Petrie 1888: 2)

His attitude to the linguistic chauvinism of his compatriots was, as might be expected, dismissive. Nor was he comfortable with the presence of dragomans among the entourage of Europeans who visited his excavations in Egypt. At Hawara, where he worked from 1887–9, one sponsor came to visit the site accompanied by 'an English manservant, a dragoman, a cook, two donkey boys and two hangers-on' (Drower 1995: 133). At Abydos, he invited the scholar and traveller Francis Galton to visit him, but specifically requested that he not bring a dragoman or other servant with him from Luxor. The reason he gave was security: fear of robbery, and of word of discoveries reaching antiquities dealers (Drower 1995: 259–60).

From the tourist's perspective, as we have already seen, there were disadvantages to having a dragoman 'interpret' Egypt and its history for them, especially on an organized package tour. Petrie was not above occasionally enjoying the comforts of travelling in style. Taking a trip on a *dhahabiya*, he compared it favourably in cultural as well as comfort terms to a journey on a Thomas Cook's steamer, which 'made few scheduled stops and when tourists were set ashore at ancient sites, little attempt was made by the dragoman to explain what they saw' (Drower 1995: 52).

In his memoir, *Ten Years' Digging in Egypt*, Petrie recommends the delights of taking a walking tour in Egypt. His advice for the traveller is of a more upbeat and practical nature than Eden's guide to *The Nile Without a Dragoman*. He insists that learning some Arabic is necessary, and also that the new arrival in Egypt, with some application, will not find it too arduous to learn enough to get by. His approach is not dissimilar to that advocated by many of the contemporary Arabic self-instruction manuals which we explored in Chapter 2. Petrie suggests a combination of advance study in England, particularly of vocabulary, and local immersion:

> Of course, the native language is as much needed as in any foreign country; but a sufficient amount of colloquial Arabic can be learned in a few weeks. Three friends of mine have come out with only what could be briefly learned in England, and each has been able in a week or two to make his way sufficiently. Learn first of all what you want in Baedecker's vocabulary; refer to Murray, or better, to a dictionary, for any further words you want; and absorb the addenda of very common words which come at the end of this chapter; then a week or two in Cairo, talking to the natives as much as possible, would quite suffice to float the active tripper. The main trouble is to catch what is said to you; and for this there is no better practice than listening to short sentences heard in the streets, and analysing them. (Petrie 1892: 187–8)

He supplies his own supplement of useful additions to the Baedeker vocabulary (Figure 8: Petrie's Addenda to Baedecker's Vocabulary).

Along the way, the traveller could also fall back on the help of locals with a smattering of English, European shopkeepers, and, in case of emergencies, 'the station-masters or post-masters can be appealed to, as they all understand

ADDENDA TO BAEDECKER'S VOCABULARY.

—◆◆—

Station, *mahatta ;* ticket, *tezkereh, warak, bilieto ;* 1st class, *brimo ;* 2nd class, *secondo ;* (does) this go to Cairo? *deh raih al Masr ?* train, *kattr ;* engine, *wabur* or *babur ;* carriage, *arabiyeh ;* goods, *buda'a ;* goods train, *kattr el buda'a ;* baggage-receipt, *bolicy* (pronounced *bolise*) *;* storage charge, *ardiyeh.* I (will) beat the telegraph (=I will telegraph), *ana adrob et telegraphia ;* the wire, *es silk.*

(The dots in the following words separate the elements, which are here translated literally.)

Show.me the snake, *warri.ni el hanesh.* Not showed.I to.him the fowl, *ma warr.et l.u.sh el farkha* (*sh* like French *pas*, untranslated). Not.thou.leave.it, *ma t.khalli.u.sh.* He opened.it, *Huweh fatah.u.* Thou camest from where? *Ente git min ayn.* From the desert (hill or plain), *min el gebel.* Thou goest where? *Ente raih fen.* Northwards, *bahri.* The engine it.leaves when? *el wabur ye.safir emta ?* at.the sunset, *fi.l maghreb.* Atest.thou five pounds in.the four.months, pound.and.quarter for the month, *kal.t khamast ertal fi.l arbat.usher, rotl.u.rub bi.sh shahr* (accent strongly as marked). Two cubits length (pair cubits) for two piastres (dual), *gozet idra bi kirshen.* Finished, *khalás.* I am very tired (I bad.ed entirely), *ana batlan khálas.* Finished entirely, *Khalás khálas.* (It) was cold very in.the.morning before the sun(rise), *kan bard kowi fi.'s subh kabl esh shems.* The peasants (are) foolish like cattle, *el fellahin maganin zeyeh behaim.* A lucky day for you (literally, day.thy, milk) *neharak leben.* By life (of) the prophet, *wa hyat en nebi.* By life (of) father.thy, *wa hyat abu.k.* Bless me! (oh peace.my) *ya salam.i* (really a title of the Deity).

Village night guard, *ghafir,* pl. *ghofera.*

Figure 8: Petrie's Addenda to Baedecker's Vocabulary (1888).

English or French. Many of them have been in Europe' (Petrie 1892: 194). Petrie offered this tip from his own personal experience in resolving problems with newly recruited members of his Egyptian workforce: 'None of them know more than a stray word or two of English so if any insurmountable difficulties should turn up I shall march all parties to Tel Barud station and get the station master to settle them, as he speaks very good English' (24 November 1884, quoted in Quirke 2010: 63).

In his insistence that it was perfectly possible for a foreign visitor to pick up functional Arabic relatively quickly, with a little application, Petrie spoke from experience – but he also held learners to high standards. His own approach was practical and industrious. His preparation before leaving for Egypt for the first time, in 1880, involved compiling Arabic vocabulary lists as well as research on the history, language and antiquities of ancient Egypt. On the voyage out, he tested his knowledge on a Moroccan fellow passenger, but 'beyond a few stray remarks on route, weather, etc., our mutual goodwill was expressed by nods, smiles and indications' (quoted in Drower 1995: 34). The difference between the dialects of Arabic spoken in Morocco and that of Egypt (and of both from the formal literary language) may have contributed to communication problems. As we shall discuss below, differences in dialect also made it difficult for archaeologists who had worked in Egypt or the Levant to switch to living and working in the other. Upon his arrival in Cairo, Petrie initially remained reliant on English-speaking Egyptians and the Arabic of James Grant ('Grant Bey'), a Scottish doctor (Quirke 2010: 52–3).

In 1881, shortly after his arrival in Cairo to begin the following year's season, Petrie was assaulted and robbed by some soldiers. The process of bringing the perpetrators to justice was frustrating: his witnesses would not testify, and the accused were prompted in court by their superior officer. However accomplished Petrie's colloquial Arabic may or may not have been by this stage, dealing with the authorities meant dealing with Turkish speakers. 'I stopped it as soon as I could by remonstrating on questioning me only through a Turk speaking French, and demanded that I should not be examined unless with an English interpreter' (Letter of 16 October 1881, quoted by Quirke 2010: 90; the incident is also recounted by Drower 1995: 49). In the end, the case came to nothing.

Over his years in Egypt and Palestine, Petrie developed a firm policy of dealing with his workers and other locals directly:

> I am accustomed to hire and pay every workman myself, and never have any interpreter with me. Nor do I believe in middlemen, and at present I have no one but workmen with me, without any overseer. Hence you will see that I do not want a staff of encumbrances about with me. (Letter discussing terms of a permit to work in Palestine, quoted in Dahlberg and O'Connell 1989: 38)

Archival material enables us to document how he developed the linguistic skills to do so. Stephen Quirke's recent study of the Egyptian workforces employed in Petrie's excavations draws on his notebooks, letters and journals to document their lives and professional careers – and, of course, Petrie's attitudes to them. The Petrie notebooks contain many transcriptions and translations of Arabic conversations, and notes made as he learns the colloquial language of different regions 'on the job'. In March 1884, in the Nile Delta, he records the things the workmen call to each other in the trenches, and his efforts to understand them and assimilate new vocabulary:

> all day the trenches echo to the shouts of 'Ya ibn el kelb! Ishtaghal Istaghal [sic], ya bint! Hawafi, ya shekh, hawafi! Ent ze hamir!' ('Oh, son of a dog! Work, work, oh daughter! Gooday, oh shekh, good day! You are like donkeys!' This *hawafi* is new to me; Ali says it is 'goodday', but he cannot explain the particular value of such a remark, and it seems to be equal to 'I've got my eye on you.') To all of which the reply contentedly, and even cheerfully, is 'Hader, ya sidi hader.' ('Ready, oh my lord, ready.') (Quoted in Quirke 2010: 61)

Further evidence of Petrie's constant efforts to improve his Arabic may be seen in the vocabulary lists which he sometimes drew up for new tasks and circumstances. In the Delta in early 1884 at the start of the first season of work at San al-Hagar, for example, he jots a list of transliterated words (without English translation) in his notebook: 'These seem to be a personal mini-vocabulary for directing the men who built a mud-brick house for Petrie as his excavation base' (Quirke 2010: 147–8). His relocation to work at Tell Hesy for the Palestine Exploration Fund was the occasion for some more lists of vocabulary in the local dialect of Arabic, for some of which he noted the Egyptian equivalents with which he was already familiar (Quirke 2010: 148–9). Petrie was also literate in Arabic, and his journals contain some writing in Arabic script, with only a couple of peculiarities of handwriting. (Quirke 2010: 147–54)

Arabic was not the only language in which Petrie needed to do business. On 20 February 1890 he wrote a letter in reasonable French to the governor of the Fayum, and the notebooks also contain a draft of a bilingual French-Arabic letter to an official in the Antiquities Service (Quirke 2010: 125–8). He records on at least one occasion that he spoke to a regional governor in Arabic, although he had heard that the latter spoke French. Evidently, he was making a point about his own familiarity with the country and its language. He also had occasion to write to the Greek consul at Zagazig and request him to take action to stop a Greek antiquities dealer who was hanging around the site: 'In case you are not able to communicate with him immediately, I should be much obliged to you to give me an order in Greek to this effect, in case he comes here again' (Quirke 2010: 128–9). The point here is perhaps as much the authority which might come from a letter in Greek from a Greek official as the dealer's ability to communicate in Arabic or any other language. Furthermore, Petrie describes being taken on a tour of the site of Oxyrhynchus by a mute local: 'Altogether we get on as well with signs as with speech' (9 December 1896, quoted in Quirke 2010: 95).

Petrie also held others to very high standards, as may be seen from the advice in his *Methods and Aims in Archaeology*. In his view 'a complete archae-ological training would require a full knowledge of history and art, a fair use of languages, and a working familiarity with many sciences' (Petrie 1904: viii), as well as ancient languages – and a field team should be expected, between them, to show competence in a wide range of these:

> The spoken language of the country should be fluently acquired for simple purposes, so as to be able to direct workmen, make bargains, and follow what is going on. To be dependent on a cook, a dragoman, or a donkey boy, is very unsafe, and prevents that close study of the workmen which is needed for making the best use of them. (Petrie 1904: 6)

T. E. Lawrence in Egypt and Syria

Long before he became 'Lawrence of Arabia', T. E. Lawrence (1888–1935) travelled the Arab world as an historian and archaeologist. He joined Petrie's field season at Kafr Ammar in Egypt in the winter of 1911–12. In his letters to friends and family, he paints a vivid picture of the eccentric great archaeologist at work:

> A Petrie dig is a thing with a flavour of its own: tinned kidneys mingle with mummy-corpses and amulets in the soup: my bed is all gritty with prehistoric alabaster jars of unique types – and my feet at night keep the bread-box from rats. For ten mornings in succession I have seen the sun rise as I breakfasted, and we come home at nightfall after lunching at the bottom of a 50-foot shaft, to draw pottery silhouettes or string bead-necklaces. In fact if I hadn't had malaria today I could make a pretty story of it all: – only then I wouldn't have time.
>
> To begin with the Professor is the great man of the camp – he's about 5' 11" high, white-haired, grey-bearded, broad and active, with a voice that split when excited and a constant feverish speed of speech; he is a man of ideas and systems, from the right way to dig a temple to the only way to clean one's teeth. Also he only is right in all things: all his subs have to take his number of sugar lumps in their tea, his species of jam with potted tongue, or be dismissed as official-bound unprogressists.
>
> Further he is easy-tempered, full of humour, and fickle to a degree that makes him delightfully quaint, and a constant source of joy and amusement in his camp. (Quoted in Drower 1995: 319–20)

In Lawrence's opinion '… what P. wants is a pedestrian intelligence to do the hackwork for him, while he does the fine things. Am awfully glad I went to him. But what a life!'.

Lawrence's previous archaeological experience had been in Syria and the Levant, to which he subsequently returned. The Egyptian interlude left him with mixed feelings, and this ambivalence was forthrightly expressed in letters to his family:

> I don't like Egypt or the Egyptians – after Carchemish and the Carchemisians – and I don't like Mrs. Petrie. He is interesting – but so intensely self-centred and self-standing. Argument etc. is ludicrous between them, for either's opinion is rooted against all winds that blow. I like him exceedingly, but rather as one thinks of a cathedral or something immovable but by earthquake. (January 18 1912)[1]

---

[1] The text of letters is taken from T. E. Lawrence Studies, www.telstudies.org; David Garnett (1938) censors a number of passages, including Lawrence's ungallant dislike of Hilda Petrie.

Among the Egyptian workers, Lawrence notes in the same letter, he was known as es-Shami 'the Syrian', and they could not understand his Syrian dialect.

Lawrence's letters give some indication of the formal efforts he made to acquire and improve his Arabic. At Oxford, before setting out to explore the Crusader castles of Syria in the summer of 1909, he took lessons from the Reverend Naser Odeh, a Syrian clergyman.[2] This was the same Rev Odeh who wrote one of the Arabic language primers discussed in Chapter 2 (Hassam and Odeh 1915), and from this we might glean some idea of the grammar, vocabulary and phrases which he taught Lawrence. He enjoyed the experience of travelling through the region on foot and without European companions, and thought that 'I have perhaps, living as an Arab with the Arabs, got a better insight into the daily life of the people than those who travel with caravan and dragomen' (letter to Sir John Rhys, Aleppo, 24 September 1909). The only other reference to dragomans I have been able to find in the Lawrence correspondence is to the dragoman of the Consul in Aleppo, from whom he had borrowed £25 to spend on antiquities. He wrote to his family to ask for money to repay him (3 August 1912, Beirut).

In the winter of 1910–11, at the American mission school in Jebail, near Beirut, Lawrence took further Arabic lessons, including reading and writing, from Miss Fareedah al-Akle (1882–1976), a Syrian schoolteacher for whom he had a great regard (Mousa 1966: 3, 5; letter to his family, Jebail, 22 January 1911; Taylor and Taylor 1964). Towards the end of her life (in a letter to one of Lawrence's biographers, John Mack, in which she was politely sceptical about the biographical project, and the cult of Lawrence), she recalled how quickly he picked up the basics of Arabic, and her impression that he was 'extremely intelligent and a good linguist' (Mack 1976: 78). They would study for an hour each day, sitting on a red sofa, Lawrence with a cat on his lap. The lessons appear to have been very congenial, and pupil and teacher had shared interests in literature, archaeology and the history of the Arabs. But Lawrence learnt and practised most of his Arabic in the field, and in particular at Carchemish.

---

[2]   Briefly mentioned by Mack (1976: 70) Rev Odeh was founder of the Anglican St Mary's Mission in
      Cairo. He died in England in 1932. His daughter, Margaret Theodosia (1887–1960), was educated
      at St Hilda's College, Oxford and campaigned for women's suffrage. She married the artist Paul Nash
      (1889–1946) in 1914, and is depicted in some of his works.

He even tried to teach a local donkey-boy (probably Dahoum, his constant companion) to read and write, asking Miss Fareedah for some books to help him (letter to Mrs. Rieder, Carchemish, 4 July 1911). In a letter of 26 June 1911, he wrote to Miss Fareedah from Carchemish with romantic notions of life among the Arabs:

> It would be rather fun living alone in one of these villages: they are all mud-built you know, and quite pleasant. And the Arabic is such amusing stuff. If I could talk it like Dahoum (by the way what does the name Dahoum mean?) you would never be tired of listening to me. (Mack 1976: 77–8. Dahoum means 'little dark one'.)

Lawrence took a certain pride in his accomplishment in Arabic, especially compared to most Europeans in the Middle East, and in being something of a 'man of the people', on familiar terms with the local workmen. In December 1911, he wrote to his mentor, the Oxford archaeologist D. G. Hogarth, describing a conversation he had had with some villagers he knew, catching up on news with them upon returning to the field. A party of German railway engineers had been working in the locale:

> All the village dropped in, and I heard all about the Germans; they put on airs – they are ignorant of antikas – not recognising a Hittite inscription; they know no language; they say sacral mento, and when we ask what they want shut, they only say it again – they drink raki all night, to two mejidies – we work seven days a week – they do no work with their hands, but sit in the tents – we may not smoke: there is no bakshish – we may not speak to them, they say it is adibsis – they cannot swim – they make a bargain and break it – Oh God the pigs, they eat crabs – and tortoises. (Letter to D. G. Hogarth, Jerablus, December 16 1911)

Lawrence also observed the difficulties an archaeologist used to working in Egypt had adjusting to a new dialect and new customs, having himself experienced the reverse:

> I am writing once again in Biredjik, to which I have come back without Woolley, to buy the roof-beams and stuffs for our house. I have written very little lately, and that hurried, but you will allow for the amount of work that falls on me with Woolley a stranger to the country, and the language and the antiquities. I have to act interpreter for him, always, though he is fairly fluent in Egyptian. ... Woolley is getting on very well – goes down with the workmen, is dropping Egyptian hauteur and ruling-race fantasies, likes Syrian cooking and sweetmeats, and

(*mirabile dictu*) our dialect! It is a pretty hard piece of work for him. (Letter to
his family, Biredjik, 20 March 1912)

In Lawrence's view the best approach a European could have was to abandon
any kind of linguistic or cultural chauvinism, and make an effort both to learn
Arabic and establish good relations with locals.

How good was Lawrence's Arabic, at the time of his early archaeological
travels, and subsequently? Given he positioned himself as a mediator (a
'dragoman', if you will) between the major players in the Arab Revolt and the
British authorities, the question has naturally arisen of the extent of his fluency.
We are in fact fortunate to have the impression of some native Arabic speakers
on his proficiency in the language – an insight which is not available to us
for most archaeologists, including Petrie. Fareedah al-Akle was one of these
observers. Suleiman Mousa, in *T. E. Lawrence: An Arab View*, interviewed a
number of other people who had known Lawrence personally, all of whom –
from participants in the Battle of Tafileh (25 January 1918) to the Emir Faisal's
private secretary at the Versailles Peace Conference, Awni Abd al-Hadi (1889–
1970) – 'unanimously agreed that as soon as Lawrence spoke one sentence of
Arabic, it was clear to all concerned that he was a foreigner' (Mousa 1966: 268):

> Lawrence was extremely sly. … He pretended that he was more Arab than
> English and that he knew Arabic as well as any Arab. But the fact is that he did
> not know Arabic all that well, but spoke it with an obvious accent. (Private letter
> from Abd al-Hadi, quoted in Mousa 1966: 227; cf. 139)

To be fair, Lawrence himself was aware that 'No easterner would ever have
taken me for an Arab for a moment' (Mousa 1966: 268); even some other
English officers were more fluent. Judging him by the standard of native
speakers – and, inevitably, of the Lawrence of Arabia legend – it is easy to be
critical. Compared to most other Europeans in the Arab world – including
most archaeologists – he was evidently a capable speaker.

Sir Leonard Woolley

Sir Charles Leonard Woolley (1880–1952), a renowned British archaeologist,
came into this profession rather by accident. He recounts that it had been

decided for him by the Warden of New College, Oxford, at the end of his last year there (Woolley 1920: 3–4). Having spent a year in Germany and France 'to get up modern languages,' he began his career as assistant keeper at the Ashmolean Museum under Sir Arthur Evans. Opportunities to work in the field soon followed.

Woolley as Archaeologist: Carchemish

The excavations of Carchemish, a Hittite city located by the village of Jerablus on the Euphrates, at that time in Turkish Syria, were first conducted by the British Museum in 1878. In 1911 the Museum decided to resume exploration of the site. A few months into the first season, Leonard Woolley was asked to assume the leadership of the team, which at the time consisted of himself and T. E. Lawrence (Fagan 1979: 226, 227; Winstone 1990: 23). He worked there from 1912 to 1914. With five seasons (1907–11) spent in Sudan before coming to Carchemish, Woolley was becoming more and more fluent in Arabic. He did not seem to be at all interested in learning Turkish.

Leonard Woolley's book entitled *Dead Towns and Living Men*, published in 1920, describes the 'incidents' of his team's work at Carchemish and offers 'some idea of native life between Aleppo and Taurus, and of what Turkish rule means there' (Woolley 1920: 7). According to an Ottoman regulation, a Turkish 'Imperial Commissaire' had to be present at the dig at all times in order to keep an eye on the process: to make sure the finds did not disappear and make it to Constantinople, 'to settle differences with local landlord, workmen, etc., and generally to see that the foreigners behave[d] themselves' (Woolley 1920: 116). In 1912, a new such official, Fuad Bey, arrived at Carchemish:

> An Arab of a good Baghdad family, he had spent all his life in Constantinople and was as much a Turk as imitation could make him – indeed, he could speak only a few words of his native Arabic. He had passed through the Civil Service College at Stamboul, and had been attached as clerical A.D.C. to the Vali of Aleppo, so as to get practical experience to fit him for the post of second-class Kaimmakam, which would be his first step on the ladder of office. He was a little fellow, about 22 years old, of mean physique, pasty-faced, and faint-hearted: he was convinced that we were out to steal every 'antika' we could lay hands on,

and would therefore make things unpleasant for him, and like a thorough-bred
city youth he looked upon Bedouins and Kurds as beasts of prey whose chief
amusement was throat-slitting. He came to us, therefore, under protest, nearly
wept when he found that he had to sleep under canvas ..., swallowed with open
mouth the stories of the ghosts that haunted the ruins, and would not go to bed
without an armed man stretched across his tent-door.

On the other hand, he was conscientious in his work and strictly honest. He
set himself to learn Arabic (for he knew no French or English), and as he talked
to the men gradually lost his fear of them. (Woolley 1920: 117)

Although filled with stories that often humorously and in a light-hearted
way describe difficulties and dangers associated with archaeological work
in the Ottoman Near East, *Dead Towns and Living Men* is of particular
interest because it contains references to interpreters and thus provides a
glimpse at the multiple roles these individuals had to take on, their social
status, and attitudes towards them. For example, Woolley tells a chilling
story of an unnamed dragoman-made-archaeologist whose presence at the
site of Jerablus, long before Woolley's time, resulted in the most devas-
tating outcome. In 1878, at the time when the British Museum first started
excavating Carchemish, the law forbidding the export of antiquities from the
Ottoman Empire did not exist. Moreover:

the scientific side of field archaeology had not been developed: one dug for
plunder wherewith to stock Museum galleries, and was interested in nothing
more than that. The monuments standing above ground at Jerablus had
attracted attention of George Smith, the father of Mesopotamian archaeology,
and the British Museum was induced to undertake the work on the site. But,
when it was simply a question of uncovering and carting away antiquities, the
presence of an archaeologist was not held necessary. The job was first offered
to Rassam, Sir Henry Layard's assistant at Nineveh, and when he refused, the
British Consul was directed to send a dragoman to carry out the work. It is not
to be wondered at that this worthy person did more harm than good; a few
broken statues and slabs covered with reliefs and inscriptions in Hittite hiero-
glyphs found their way to London, but fragments of these very pieces remained
in situ undiscovered, or were thrown into the rubbish-heaps, trenches were
driven through standing walls, parts of the great palace stairway were pulled
up, and sculptures not seemed worthy of removal were left exposed upon the
ground to be cut up into mill-stones or mutilated by idle villagers. We can
only be thankful that the dragoman, liking little his surroundings or his work,

reported adversely on the latter's prospects, and after a short time left the Kala'at again in peace. (Woolley 1920: 158–9)

When Woolley was working at Carchemish, he employed a very different kind of interpreter. Haj Wahid, a 'legendary figure with a turbulent character', used to serve as *kavass* (an armed courier accompanying the travellers) at the British Consulate at Aleppo, and considered 'therefore that he owes to the English an allegiance which far outweighs his duties as an Ottoman subject' (Woolley 1920: 96). However, after a somewhat disturbing incident – Haj Wahid killed four and badly wounded one of the six men who tried to get back at him for seducing their sister – he was sent to prison for three years. The British Consul later remarked that 'one murder or two might have been overlooked, but four in a night was too much of a good thing and [he] had to let the law take its course' (Woolley 1920: 99). Nevertheless, when the Carchemish expedition had begun, it was the Consulate that recommended Haj Wahid as 'a servant, and he was engaged as cook, dragoman, and general factotum, nor has he failed to give full satisfaction' (Woolley 1920: 99).

Despite Haj Wahid's turbulent nature, he seemed to have been devoted to Woolley and they got along famously:

> He is dragoman, ready to act as interpreter, to drive a bargain, to ride out on messages, or to entertain guests in our absence, and generally to protect our interests. (Woolley 1920: 100)

Haj Wahid also turned out to be irreplaceable in dealing with the Turkish authorities. Having received a rejection to their application to excavate at Jerablus, Woolley and Lawrence decided to go and talk to the *kaimmakam* (the Governor) in person. They were accompanied by their 'cook and major-domo, Haj Wahid, who was to act as interpreter should Turkish be required' (Woolley 1920: 152), as both Woolley and Lawrence could manage the Arabic. The conversation turned out to be not as amicable as they hoped.

> At the start Haj Wahid had to act as interpreter, for the Turk knew only a few words of French, and, though he could speak Arabic, began by pretending he could not: it was only when the interview grew more exciting that he and I both dropped into Arabic and dispensed with the third person. (Woolley 1920: 153)

They did not come to an agreement at the time and had to return the next day. Once again, they were escorted by

> Haj Wahid, in his role of interpreter once more, tricked out in his best clothes, with two revolvers stuck in the voluminous folds of his silk sash and a carbine over his shoulder to add to his importance. (Woolley 1920: 167)

Yet again, the Governor was obstinate and proclaimed Woolley's permit to be invalid. Even the official letters from the former project director and from the British Museum did not change the situation. Since all these documents were in English, and the Governor did not understand English, they simply would not do. Woolley offered to translate the documents into French, and further suggested that a French-speaking interpreter working at the office of the *kaimmakam* might be called in to translate them into Turkish from French.

> 'I should not trust such translation,' replied the *kaimmakam*; 'until the British Museum issues this order in Turkish I shall pay no attention to it'. (Woolley 1920: 153–5)

At this point, Woolley felt that some drastic measures were called for and quite literally put a gun to the *kaimmakam*'s head. This proved to be rather effective and the Governor agreed to allow the work to begin the next day. He also agreed to write an order to the *onbashi* (a corporal responsible for security of the site) and did so, of course, in Turkish. Woolley, not being certain of the content, asked the Governor to send for an interpreter who would then translate it into French. Perhaps the *kaimmakam* had a change of heart or perhaps it was the gun that Woolley still held in his hand, but 'the interpreter duly came and the order was found to be correct' (Woolley 1920: 157). Although Haj Wahid was present the whole time, he was never asked to examine the document in Turkish produced by the Governor. Instead, the services of an 'official' interpreter were required. It is quite possible that Haj Wahid was illiterate and could not have helped with a written translation. On the other hand, it seems apparent that Haj Wahid's role was never simply that of an interpreter – essentially he was a bodyguard, 'a mediator with guns' – and must have had quite a formidable presence armed with his revolvers and a carbine. This colourful character, a significant figure of Woolley's entourage, undoubtedly added to his master's prestige at the Governor's office – both visually and psychologically.

Woolley at Ur

In 1922, Leonard Woolley was put in charge of excavations at Ur, a joint venture between the British Museum and the University of Pennsylvania that lasted for twelve glorious seasons. Because of its close association with the Old Testament, the site held a particular attraction for Woolley. Having been trained as a theologian, he dreamed of bringing the holy text to life:

> It was always Woolley's hope to discover some references to Abraham and although this name never appeared in the cuneiform record he succeeded in reconstructing the background of that Old Testament prophet's original home before he migrated from Sumer (later named Babylonia) to Palestine. (Mallowan 2001: 34)

With all his time spent in the field at Carchemish and later on the slow march from Kut el Amara to Kastamuni and then to Kedos as a prisoner of war, Leonard Woolley's Arabic had improved significantly. In May 1924, after three seasons at Ur, before the startling discovery of the treasures of the cemetery, he was invited to Baghdad by Gertrude Bell (Director of Antiquities in Iraq at the time) to give a lecture before an important audience that consisted of 'Arab notables and high-ranking officers of the British High Commission' (Winstone 1990: 128). This talk was given at a politically important moment, namely at the time when Iraq's new constitution was being drafted, and Woolley made savvy political choices to emphasize the new-found independence of the ancient land of Iraq in order to stroke the nationalistic pride of the members of his audience. Gertrude Bell was very pleased with the presentation. Woolley spoke in English and Arabic and 'his enthusiasm, conveyed in a torrent of English and Arabic, left his audience spellbound' (Winstone 1990: 128).

Yet not all scholars working in the Near East were able to master spoken Arabic. Father S. J. Burrows, a Jesuit priest from Campion Hall, who worked with Woolley at Ur as his epigraphist, presented a peculiar example of such 'linguistic ineptitude':

> although well versed in ancient Oriental languages, Sumerian, Babylonian, Phoenician, Aramaic and Hebrew, ... [he] was unable to bend his mind to the vernacular and had the greatest difficulty in asking for a jar of hot water in Arabic. (Mallowan 2001: 39)

The First World War: Woolley as Spy

Sometime in 1911–12, D. G. Hogarth, a British archaeologist who worked with Woolley in Carchemish, wrote a report to the director of the British Museum, Sir Frederic Kenyon, mentioning a particular meeting in Constantinople. One of the people present at that meeting was Gerald Fitzmaurice, the chief dragoman of the British embassy, who was closely linked to 'the secret service organization established in the Mediterranean by Admiral Lord Fisher through "the patriotism of several magnificent Englishmen"' (Winstone 1990: 27–8). It is not at all surprising that bi- or multi-lingual individuals living and working in the Near East would occasionally be recruited to participate in extracurricular activities: in other words, they were often officially or unofficially employed by the secret services. The archaeologists, too, with their knowledge of land, customs and languages, as well as personal connections among the locals, proved quite useful at the time of war (see Allen 2011). In the words of Leonard Woolley:

> the war brought the archaeologist out in a new light, and his habit of prying about in countries little known, his knowledge of peoples, and his gift of tongues, were turned to uses far other than his wont. In Egypt alone there were half-a-dozen of us attached to the Headquarters Staff; in Mesopotamia, in the Greek islands and at the Salonica, there were intelligence officers and interpreters who had graduated in archaeology, and the discovery that what had seemed the mere stock-in-trade of one's profession could thus find wider scope made one regard it as possessing maybe some value of its own (Woolley 1920: 6–7).

In late November of 1915, when Gertrude Bell travelled from Cairo to Port Said, she was met there by Leonard Woolley, who, in the rank of Captain, was the 'head in the Intelligence Department at Port Said' (Bell 1927, vol. 1, 30 November 1915). Indeed, with the outbreak of the First World War Woolley served as an intelligence officer posted to Cairo, until the Turks took him prisoner late in 1916 when his ship blew up in the eastern Mediterranean.

Woolley as Prisoner of War in 1914–1916

A is for Askar, a taciturn folk
Who limit their language to Yessak and Yok.
I's for Interpreters, genial Greeks,
Heavily perfumed with garlic and leeks.
Y is for Yassak – a curious word
Employed by the Arab, the Turk, and the Kurd.
(Woolley 1921: 1–2)

'Ingleze chok fenner' = 'English very bad' (Woolley 1921: 179)

Information about Leonard Woolley's experience as a prisoner of war and his interactions with, as well as observations on, numerous interpreters in the prison camps comes from yet another book. *From Kastamuni to Kedos, Being a Record of Experiences of Prisoners of War in Turkey, 1916–1918* appeared in 1921 and is said to have been 'written by many hands and edited by C. L. Woolley (Capt. R.F.A.)'. It claims to present a compilation of reactions and thoughts of Woolley himself and of other prisoners of war – gathered by him and published by Basil Blackwell, a friend of the Woolley family for two gener-ations. In the introduction, Woolley states that this book is 'merely a record of our prison camps'. Seventy or so officers were transferred on foot, first from Kut el Amara to Kastamuni, and then from Kastamuni to Kedos. Kastamuni, located about 100 miles north-east of Ankara, was a Turkish prisoners of war base to which Woolley and several other fellow officers were sent (Winstone 1990: 81). Kedos (Geddos), their destination, was on the rail line from Afion to Smyrna.

Learning foreign languages seems to have been one of the pastimes Woolley and other officers would engage in while stationed in a camp: for that, they organized a number of lectures and classes. For example, Woolley took such an improvised class in Italian, whereas other officers 'took Russian, Arabic, modern Greek, Tamil, Burmese and Turkish' (Winstone 1990: 86). The latter proved useful and, on a rare occasion when interpreters were nowhere to found or were not provided, Woolley's fellow officer, Captain Spackman, was able to act 'as interpreter for the new arrivals' albeit 'with his limited knowledge of Turkish' (Woolley 1921: 63, 82).

It emerges from Woolley's book that the interpreters seem to have been a constant presence in the prison camps and on the march. As a group, they are routinely mentioned among others, such as Turkish officers and askars: 'stories told by Sherif Bey, by the interpreters, by well-informed townsfolk and by the posters of the guard ...' (Woolley 1921: 3, 8, 41). One is immediately reminded of Herodotus' reference to numerous interpreters in Egypt – he took them to be a particular class of the Egyptian society, along with the cowherds, swineherds, shopkeepers, boatmen, warriors and priests (Herod. II.164 [trans. Waterfield 1998]). A drawing of a short and plump man – perhaps a caricatured collective image of the interpreters encountered in the camps – and inscribed '"Napoleon," our interpreter at Kastamuni' (Figure 9), serves as a vignette for the *From Kastamuni to Kedos*.

Overall, the interpreters encountered by Woolley and his fellow inmates in the camps and on the march are derogatorily described as physically unpleasant, stupid, ignorant and lazy, often neglecting their duties and spending most of their time at the tric-trac board (Woolley 1921: 3). Moreover, they seemed always to be ready to take advantage of the prisoners – and such opportunities presented themselves repeatedly:

> At first we were only allowed to write four postcards and two letters a month, all of four lines, and at first p.c.'s were only obtainable by buying them from a rascally interpreter. (Woolley 1921: 6)

The imprisoned officers also had to rely on the camp interpreters for news of the outside world:

> The spring season indeed gave birth to a wonderful crop of rumours. We were told that we were all to be moved to Broussa to replace repatriated Russian officers; the new interpreter, a Greek Ottoman Jew, assured us that Damascus had been taken months before. (Woolley 1921: 92)

Throughout Woolley's narrative the linguistic and even mental abilities of the men serving as interpreters are questioned and ridiculed persistently. When a group of prisoners arrived at Kastamuni, a 'new Commandant – a moth-eaten dugout *kaimmakam*' communicates with the officers 'through the interpreter, a miserable-looking Greek', presumably translating from Turkish into English (Woolley 1921: 3). One day, the rules of conduct in Kastamuni, translated from Turkish to English by the interpreters on hand, were posted around

" NAPOLEON," OUR INTERPRETER AT KASTAMUNI.

Figure 9: '"Napoleon," our interpreter at Kastamuni,' from Woolley 1921: viii.

the camp. These caused much anger and provided some comic relief as well, 'thanks to the ignorance of our interpreters':

> To the Prisoners of War at Kastamuni: 1. The officers allowed to sit on the
> trenches that are founded near the door of the school and in the higher place

that is opposite the school upon the fountain. 2. If any officers are not obeying the centeries the century will have the permission to strike with his steak and with his rifles.

Naturally, 'this latter order made us all very angry at the time, and on Colonel Annesley's remonstrating with the Commandant as to allowing his men to strike officers he apologized and the notice was removed' (Woolley 1921: 14). Yet another derogatory remark is found in the account of a performance by a makeshift Pierrot troupe consisting of imprisoned officers organized by Colonel Taylor in one of the camps. In addition to the prisoners of war, this performance attracted the attention of the camp's Commandant and his Turkish guests, who were perhaps surprisingly described as 'uncomprehending but resolutely civilized'. During the performance, it appears that they were 'feverishly assisted by the whispered explanation of a garlic-breathing interpreter understanding less, if possible, than his masters' (Woolley 1921: 127).

Overall, one gets an impression that the interpreters that surrounded Woolley and other prisoners of war in the camps and on the march were regarded by them as inferior beings, and were despised more than the Turkish governmental and army officials. It is perhaps noteworthy that nowhere in the text do we encounter a Turk or an Arab serving as an interpreter. It seems that this role was allocated to the Greeks and 'Greek Ottoman Jews' (members of the Greek-speaking Jewish communities). Their marginal status within the Ottoman Empire was possibly augmented by the marginal status of interpreters – the go-betweens that under the circumstances had to facilitate communication between the Ottoman officials and the British officers amidst the war, a most disagreeable combination indeed.

Max Mallowan and Agatha Christie

This section falls somewhere in between those dealing with tourists and archaeologists journeying through and exploring Egypt and the Levant. Agatha Christie (1890–1976), the most popular mystery writer of the twentieth century (if not of all time), first travelled to the Middle East as a young debutante. She was seventeen when her mother decided to spend the winter season in Cairo. With practically no money left in the family after the death of Agatha's father, Egypt, with its Anglophone community and balls and dancers, provided a much more affordable alternative to London. At the time, young Agatha was preoccupied with new dresses and concerned with parties and social life; the beauties of Egypt went unnoticed. She began discovering the true splendours of the Orient only twenty years later, when she toured Egypt and the Near East, and eventually visited the site of ancient Ur in 1928 (Christie 2010: 199, 204). It was there that she met a young archaeologist, Max Mallowan, who soon became her husband.

Sir Max Edgar Lucien Mallowan (1904–78), a prominent British archaeologist, was appointed a junior staff member and assistant to Leonard Woolley at Ur, immediately after graduating from Oxford. Trained as a classicist and with no background in Ancient Mesopotamia, Mallowan was given this position 'with the understanding that … [he] would serve as general field assistant and would be taught the job by Woolley' (Mallowan 2001: 40). In addition, he was expected to quickly 'learn Arabic and become reasonably proficient at the spoken language'. He claimed to have never been 'a good linguist':

> but by dint of keeping Van Ess's grammar in my pocket for several years on end I became tolerably competent in the speaking and understanding of it and at eliciting sense by a dialectic method of question and answer, which stood me in good stead during the war when better Arabists than I were often unable to put their Arabic across. (Mallowan 2001: 40)

'Van Ess's grammar' referred to by Mallowan was none other than *The Spoken Arabic of Mesopotamia*, a book that has not lost its importance to this day (Van Ess 1917; Bergman 1982: 193). The author, Dr John Van Ess (1879–1949), was a missionary for the Dutch Reformed Church of America, who had lived in Iraq since 1902. A man with extraordinary linguistic and diplomatic abilities, fluent in Arabic and Turkish (Bergman 1982; Van Ess 1974: 4, 27), he received a thorough grounding in Arabic grammar and reading at Princeton. Once in Iraq, Van Ess had to apply his 'book learning' to mastering the spoken word, '… After a few months in a completely Arab environment he was speaking "the language of the angels" as though it was his own' (Van Ess 1974: 27). Knowledge of Arabic, which according to some had 'all the dignity of Latin, the variety of English, the beauty of Italian, the sonority of German, the flexibility of Greek and the bewilderment of Russian' (Van Ess 1974: 23), was essential for archaeologists working in the Near East and for 'anyone who wanted to win the friendship and confidence of the Arabs, in towns or tribes' (Van Ess 1974: 27).

Nevertheless, when travelling or working in the area, assistance and support from the locals could not be underestimated. When, in 1932, Mallowan and his wife embarked on a three-month-long survey expedition through Syria in order to look for possible excavation sites, Hamoudi ibn Sheikh Ibrahim, 'a guide, philosopher, and friend' accompanied them (Christie Mallowan 1999: 69). Hamoudi was a native of Jerablus in North Syria and had worked for Woolley at Carchemish, before coming to Ur as a foreman (Mallowan 2001: 43). In the course of this trip it was Mallowan who negotiated food and hotels. Hamoudi was quietly present at all times, examining the accommodations and advising the best course of action; he also served as 'ambassador', hiring workmen (Christie Mallowan 1999: 70).

According to Christie, Max Mallowan already spoke rather fluent Arabic and some Persian when they met in 1928. He conversed with the workmen and sheikhs, and often interpreted for Agatha (Christie Mallowan 1999: 32, 111). Occasionally, in the matters of 'public relations' with the neighbouring Arab tribes, spousal teamwork was required: once, a local sheikh brought several of his wives with health issues to the expedition camp. It was up to Agatha Christie to examine them and then to describe their conditions and suggest possible treatments to Mallowan, who, standing outside the hut (where the examination took place), conveyed this information to the sheikh positioned nearby (Christie Mallowan 1999: 136). Despite all her travels and fieldwork in the area, Agatha's Arabic never became fluent. By the third (and last) season in Syria, she claimed to understand one word in seven when rapid Arabic was spoken. Her basic spoken Arabic consisted 'almost entirely of phrases like "This is not clean. Do it like this. Do not use that cloth. Bring in tea," and such domestic orders' (Christie Mallowan 1999: 189). This might have been enough to get by with in the expedition camp, but, when on a number of occasions 'friendly Kurdish women' approached Agatha and attempted to converse with her, she could not respond, although she seems to have understood a few basic things (Christie Mallowan 1999: 90).

Robin Macartney, a young architect who accompanied Mallowan and Christie on their three-month-long surveying tour through Syria, and who later participated in the excavations at Chagar Bazar, seemed to have been unable or unwilling 'to risk a word of Arabic' (Christie Mallowan 1999: 71). One morning:

> Hamoudi says sadly to Max that he has talked long and earnestly to the Khwaja Macartney last night, but alas, not even now, after two months, does the Khwaja Mac understand a word of Arabic! Max asks Mac how he is getting on with Van Ess's spoken Arabic. Mac replies that he seems to have mislaid it. (Christie Mallowan 1999: 64)

When Macartney returned for the second season at Chagar Bazar, the foremen ran over to him and greeted him in Arabic:

> Mac, as usual, responds in English. 'Ah, the Khwaja Mac!' sighs Alawi. 'Still will it be necessary for him to whistle for all he wants!' (Christie Mallowan 1999: 166)

Whistling, apparently, being the preferred (or the only possible) way of communication between Macartney and the Arabs working at the dig. Numerous references to multi-lingual communication involving tourists and archaeologists in Egypt and the Near East can be found in Agatha Christie's novels set in the Orient. Undoubtedly, these were inspired by the author's own experiences in both capacities. In 1936, the Mallowans returned to dig at Chagar Bazar. In the same year Christie wrote *Murder in Mesopotamia*, a mystery that takes place on an archaeological dig in Iraq. It was dedicated to her 'many archaeological friends in Iraq and Syria', who would probably have recognized in the murder victim, Louise Leidner, wife of the director, some personal characteristics of 'the formidable Katharine Woolley', the infamous wife of Leonard Woolley, Mallowan's former director at Ur (Osborne 1982: 135, 137). In the text there are several references to the different abilities and inclinations of members of the archaeological team to speak Arabic. For example, an assistant to the director, Mr. Emmet, an American, a character that was loosely based on Max Mallowan, speaks fluent Arabic and holds several animated conversations with the workmen and a house-boy (Christie 2001a: 66). A British doctor who has been living in the area for several years, is also described as fluent in Arabic (Christie 2001a: 115). Several team members whose Arabic has much room for progress, make efforts to carry out conversations with the locals in order to improve it (Christie 2001a: 82).

In 1937, Agatha Christie accompanied her husband to Syria once again – this time they were excavating at Tell Brak (Osborne 1982: 146). However, her writing interests took her to another exotic place – Egypt. That year she wrote and published two books: a play set in pharaonic Egypt and an Hercule Poirot murder mystery set in modern Egypt (Osborne 1982: 146). The principal part of *Death on the Nile* takes place on an old river-steamer, S.S. Karnak, that travels between the First and Second Cataracts of the Nile. This exotic venue allows for a perfect and intimate setting for a murder mystery with no more than fifteen *dramatis personae*. The characters depicted in the story undoubtedly could have been encountered in such a setting: a German tourist, who would not let go of his copy of the Baedeker, 'reading sonorously in German' from it, 'pausing every now and then to translate for the benefit' of a young American woman; an Italian archaeologist who prefers to examine the reliefs without interruption while 'disdaining the remarks of the dragoman' (Christie 2001b: 56, 62, 63, 64). Once, an 'official' dragoman makes an appearance, calling the group to order, taking charge and leading the party ashore to visit Abu Simbel (Christie 2001b: 63).

In Agatha Christie's *Appointment with Death*, written and published in 1938, the story begins in Jerusalem and moves to Petra, following several British and American tourists touring the Land of the Bible. Hercule Poirot appears on the scene only after the murder has been committed. Servants, guides and a dragoman are a constant presence throughout the novel. It soon becomes apparent that all the references to a dragoman actually point towards the same character, who accompanies the group on a tour of and around Jerusalem and eventually goes with them to Petra. As the story develops, many passing commentaries allow us to paint a fuller picture of this rather unpleasant – so we are led to believe – individual. He is constantly described as 'fat' and 'voluble', 'talking … with quite unintelligible fluency' (Christie 2001c: 26, 48, 53). His ardent anti-Semitic views and constant 'anti-Zionist lamentations' and rants about 'the iniquities of Jews' irritate the members of the group and even 'fray [their] nerves to a frazzle' (Christie 2001c: 53, 56). Moreover, Mahmoud's competence as a guide comes under suspicion, as his stories were deemed 'grossly inaccurate' and 'misleading', at least compared with the trusted Baedeker that several tourists have on hand (Christie 2001c: 91). Dealing with clients that constantly contradict you out of Baedeker and find 'fault with the type of bed provided' must be exhausting even for 'the pestilential dragoman'; according to him, good-tempered tourists are rather rare (Christie 2001c: 60, 131). One such member of the group who seems to be 'unaccountably in good temper' converses with him during their excursion up the mountain in Petra:

> ... panting a little, [she] asked the dragoman, Mahmoud, who, in spite of his ample proportions, showed no signs of distress: 'Don't you ever have trouble getting people up there? Elderly ones, I mean.' 'Always, we always have trouble', agreed Mahmoud serenely. 'Do you always try and take them?' Mahmoud shrugged his thick shoulders. 'They like to come. They have paid money to see them. The Bedouin guides are very clever – very sure-footed – always they manage'. (Christie 2001c: 61)

Mahmoud the dragoman does much more than just provide 'inaccurate' information on the sites. He accompanies the group at all times, arranges for transport and communicates with numerous Bedouin servants attached to the camp at Petra. The latter are referred to as 'my poor desert mutts' by Colonel Carbury, a representative of the British Army in Transjordania (Christie 2001c: 131, 161). In addition, Mahmoud takes care of the everyday routine, such as arranging teas and meals and dispatching servants to attend to the guests (Christie 2001c: 92, 96).

In the course of his murder investigation at Petra, Hercule Poirot eventually has to question Mahmoud. It is from this interview (which is more of a monologue) that curious snippets of the dragoman's daily practices, inclinations and aspirations become apparent:

> The stout dragoman was voluble. Words dripped from him in a rising flood. 'Always, always, I am blamed. When anything happens, say, always, my fault. Always my fault. When Lady Ellen Hunt sprain her ankle coming down from Place of Sacrifice it my fault, though she would go high-heeled shoes and she sixty at least – perhaps seventy. My life all on misery! Ah! What with miseries and iniquities, Jews to us ... ... Half-past five o'clock, you say? No, I not thinks any servants were about then. You see, lunch is late – two o'clock. And then to clear it away. After lunch all afternoon sleep. We all settle sleep by half-past three. At five I who am soul of efficiency – always – always I watch for the comfort of ladies and gentleman. I came knowing that time all English ladies want tea. But no one there. For me, that is very well – better than usual. I can go back to sleep. Naturally the boys would not tell. Abdul say it Mohammed, and Mohammed say it Aziz and Aziz say it Aissa, and so on. They are all very stupid Bedouin – understand nothing'. (Christie 2001c: 116–17)

Naturally, he, Mahmoud, understands everything and considers himself a rather educated man:

> He took a breath and continued: 'Now, I have advantage of Mission education. I recite you Keats – Shelley – "Iadadoveandasweedovedied – ."' Poirot flinched. Though English was not his native tongue, he knew it well enough to suffer from the strange enunciation of Mahmoud. 'Superb!' He said hastily. 'Superb! Definitely I recommend you to all my friends.' He contrived to escape from the dragoman's eloquence. (Christie 2001c: 116–17)

Now, what did the great detective actually miss? 'Iadadoveandasweedovedied' – this seemingly unintelligible line can be identified as indeed belonging to a 1818 poem entitled 'Song', by John Keats (Keats 1848: 260):

> I had a dove and the sweet dove died;
> And I have thought it died of grieving:
> O, what could it grieve for? Its feet were tied,
> With a silken thread of my own hand's weaving;
> Sweet little red feet! why should you die –
> Why should you leave me, sweet bird! why?
> You lived alone in the forest tree,
> Why, pretty thing! would you not live with me?
> I kissed you oft and gave you white peas:
> Why not live sweetly, as in the green trees?

The highly comical effect of the scene was undoubtedly achieved by an unlikely juxtaposition of a very large foreign man and an extremely sentimental and quintessentially English Romantic poem. Whether Keats' 'Song' is an allusion to loss of a loved one as experienced by an overbearingly possessive lover, or whether it is indeed about the death of a little bird is of no consequence here. This enormous dissonance in cultures, sensibilities, and, ultimately, languages provides ample reason for a hearty chuckle. Most probably, this humorous episode was based on a real-life occurrence. Having met at Ur, Mallowan was asked by Katharine Woolley to accompany Agatha Christie on her journey through the Middle East, which he did. While they were staying at Kerbala:

> a policeman who was only speaking Arabic with Max, all of a sudden broke the silence and said: 'Hail to thee, blithe spirit! Bird thou never wert.' I looked at him, startled. He proceeded to finish the poem. 'I learned that,' he said, nodding his head. 'Very good, in English.' I said it was very good. That seemed to end that

part of the conversation. I should never have envisaged myself coming all the way to Iraq so as to have Shelley's 'Ode to a Skylark' recited to me by an Iraqi policeman in an Eastern garden at midnight. (Christie 2010: 481)

Additionally, there might have been more poetry recited that night. In his memoirs Max Mallowan briefly referred to the same episode: apparently, the same policeman also recited 'Twinkle, Twinkle Little Star' in Arabic (Mallowan 2001: 45).

In the years between the second decade of the nineteenth century and the outbreak of the First World War, numerous British and American Christian missions were established throughout the Arab world (Van Ess 1974: xi). Although the roles and goals of these missions varied, depending on the political situation in a particular region, many of them opened schools that were trying to attract the natives. These schools were certainly part of a rather superficial attempt to 'Europeanize' the Arabs (Bergman 1982: 183), hence the mechanical memorization of poems by Shelley and Keats. On the other hand, having a better command of English and cursory understanding of the Anglophone culture gave the Arabs more employment opportunities (see Bergman 1982: 186), in particular in the tourist industry.

In 1945, seven years after *Appointment with Death* was published as a novel, Agatha Christie turned it into a play. Certain significant changes were introduced, the main one being the removal of Hercule Poirot from the cast of characters. Interestingly, the role of Mahmoud the dragoman had been built up in order to provide 'the conventional comic relief, which used to be thought necessary in plays of this kind' (Osborne 1982: 162). With large numbers of tourists travelling to Egypt and Mesopotamia in the first half of the twentieth century the figure of the dragoman became a cultural cliché, a necessary and ever-present stock character. Often a target for jokes, perceived as a constant nuisance, dragomans, despite their ability to speak the same language as tourists, fundamentally remained 'the other' – beings that were particularly easy to demonize. 'I suppose Mr Mah Mood – I cannot remember his name – but the dragoman, I mean, I suppose he could not be a Bolshevik agent?' (Christie 2001c: 131), inquires one of the British tourists in *Appointment with Death*.

4

Americans in the 'Land of the Bible'

The Wolfe Expedition

There are also at Baghdad the men ... who still collect, by means of Arabs digging in graves, the gold, tablets, cylinders, and other objects to be found in the mounds. A considerable quantity of these objects find their way from Baghdad to Europe every year, and we are fortunate in being able to bring home a collection of them. (Ward 1885: 57)

The country today has all been uncultivated and barren, and yet this is the site of the Garden of Eden, and this is of unsurpassed fertility, and would be teeming with population if there were a good government. What a region for colonization! (Ward 1898: 351)

In the second half of the nineteenth century American academia saw a rapidly growing interest in the languages and archaeology of the Ancient Near East. Exciting accounts of travels and ruins in Babylonia, Nineveh and Nimrud, published in the early 1850s by Sir Austen Henry Layard, a great traveller, romantic archaeologist and cuneiformist, gave Americans a taste for exploring the mystical land of the Bible.[1] Correlations made between the archaeological remains and the passages from the Old Testament, in the words of Hermann V. Hilprecht, a German-born professor of Assyriology and Semitic Philology at the University of Pennsylvania, 'appealed at once to the religious sentiment and to the general intelligence of the people' (Hilprecht 1903: 290). The Ancient Near East was becoming even more tangible, as Mesopotamian antiquities were beginning to trickle into the country. American missionaries who resided throughout the Near East were sending assorted archaeological

---

[1] Forthcoming book by Andrew Oliver (Oliver 2014) deals with the American visitors to Egypt in the earlier period, from 1774 to 1839. We are grateful to Christopher Lightfoot for this reference.

items to their *almae matres*, such as Andover Theological Seminary, Bowdoin College, Middlebury College, Yale, to name but a few (Meade 1974: 21–2). In May 1859, it was announced that the 'Nineveh Marbles,' a selection of thirteen sculptures, given to the New York Historical Society by the 'munificent' James Lenox, a well-known bibliophile and philanthropist, had finally arrived and had been 'placed in the Refectory' (*The Historical Magazine* 1859: 146).

The bourgeoning fascination with 'the lands of Ashurbanapal and Nebuchadnezzar' manifested itself in the creation of a number of learned societies in the United States, such as the American Oriental Society (1842) and the Society of Biblical Literature and Exegesis (1880). The recently established Archaeological Institute of America (1879) shared these interests. 'England and France have done a noble work in Assyria and Babylonia. It is time for America to do her part. Let us send an American Expedition,' – such was the main idea put forward in the spring 1884 at the meetings of the American Oriental Society and the Society of Biblical Exegesis and Archaeology (Ward 1886: 5; Hilprecht 1903: 290). Hence, an expedition had been organized, which bore the name of Miss Catherine Lorillard Wolfe, of New York City, who singlehandedly contributed the $5,000 required for this undertaking (Ward 1886: 6).

The main purpose of the Wolfe Expedition was as a reconnaissance mission, including preliminary survey, photographing the ruins and the landscapes, as well as investigating 'the practicability of further excavations there' and finding promising sites (Ward 1886: 5). The expedition reports reveal additional goals, namely 'learning what is now to be found in the hands of the local collectors of antiquities, and what might be at once secured for our museums' (Ward 1886: 7). With the 'Oriental tablets fever' spreading from Europe to America, the notion that 'the collections of these small and inconspicuous written monuments … [were] of first importance' seems to have been imposed on the members of the expedition by their colleagues on both sides of the Atlantic, and they were urged to make 'special inquiries as to the chief sources of supply of the tablets and other similar objects which are continually finding their way to Europe' (Ward 1886: 6). However, the team neither had permission to excavate nor had any plans to do so.

In September 1884, the expedition was on its way. Dr William Hayes Ward, a clergyman, educator, Orientalist, active member of the American

Oriental Society and of the Society of Biblical Literature, and, at the time, one of the editors of the *Independent*, was appointed the director. He left the United States on 6 September 1884, and, having stopped for scholarly consultations in London, Paris, Munich, Vienna and Budapest, arrived safely at Constantinople. There he met one member of his team, Mr J. H. Haynes, then an instructor in Robert College (Constantinople), who had served as photographer with the Assos Expedition. The second member of the Wolfe Expedition, Dr J. R. S. Sterrett, of the American School at Athens, was waiting for them in Smyrna. Although, according to William H. Ward, both men 'possessed sufficient command of the Turkish language' (Ward 1886: 9), a fourth individual, 'who was to act as attendant and interpreter,' also joined the team (Ward 1886: 9). It is worth noting that, in the published official expedition reports, keeping up with what seems to be a universal tradition of anonymity and invisibility of interpreters throughout the centuries, Ward simply refers to him as a 'young man' (Ward 1886: 9). This young man's identity becomes apparent in later references to the Wolfe expedition: it was Daniel Z. Noorian, who, on one occasion, was fleetingly described as 'an intelligent Armenian' (Hilprecht 1903: 290). A native of Sert, an Ottoman subject and a Christian, Daniel Zado Noorian was hired by Dr Ward in Constantinople,[2] where the latter had to spend a much longer time than initially expected, waiting for the *firman* for the Wolfe Expedition. The difficulties in obtaining the said document were apparently caused by a curious linguistic misunderstanding that involved an official interpreter of the Sublime Porte. Despite the fact that the 'American Secretary of State had instructed the American Minister there [in Constantinople] to ask for such *firman*,' it was refused twice. The source of the problem was a mistake in the Turkish rendition of the documents:

> twice the interpreter attached to the Porte had translated the word 'exploration' by a term implying excavation … But long and patient explanation had finally made it clear that no excavation was intended. (Ward 1886: 7–8)[3]

Although the Wolfe Expedition 'strictly obeyed the directions of the Turkish government' and did not attempt any digging, Dr Ward acknowledged that 'a

---

[2] Meade (1974: 51) mistakenly states that Noorian joined the Wolfe Expedition in Baghdad.
[3] On interpreters working with the Porte, see Lewis 2004: Chapters 2 and 15; Panzac 1997: 451–76; Kuneralp 1997: 479–83; Mansel 1996: 133–62.

fine collection of Assyrian and Babylonian antiquities can be made without waiting for a *firman* to excavate' (Ward 1886: 32). The locals, having worked on many earlier digs and thus having acquired the necessary skills to hunt for antiquities in general and for the much coveted tablets in particular, had become tireless suppliers to the ever-growing antiquities market, the British Museum alone purchasing 'some thousands of dollars worth of tablets' (Ward 1886: 33). According to Ward, 'it was not too late for America to compete with Europe for these collections', which at the time were considered the main vehicles for encouraging and developing 'scholarship of a country' (Ward 1886: 33). In fact, he saw as his mission to obtain 'or opening the way for obtaining, for America, the monuments of Babylonian literature and art'; in order to do that, he had to 'find out what antiquities are being found and offered for sale' – by putting himself 'in communication with every man' – 'Christian, Jew, or Moslem' – 'who dealt in antiquities' (Ward 1886: 31). As a result, Ward managed to bring back:

> an excellent collection of small engraved and inscribed objects in gold, chalcedony, lapis lazuli, and clay, burnt and unburnt. ... They form an excellent beginning for a collection, superior to any yet obtained for this country. (Ward 1886: 31)

His desire was to place these pieces, 'at their first cost, in the Metropolitan Museum' (Ward 1886: 32).

Dr Ward makes several casual references to interpreters in his published reports. For example, he describes the caravan of the expedition as follows:

> ... [it] consisted, besides ourselves and the interpreter taken at Constantinople, of a Moslem for general service, but specially charged with the care of our riding horses, a cook and two muleteers, seven horses, five mules, and a donkey. (Ward 1886: 10)

On their journey throughout Babylonia, Ward would break away from the caravan, and take with him 'an interpreter and a guide' or 'a soldier and interpreter', as he visited 'some mound off from our route' or 'Tel Ibrahim' (Ward 1886: 19, 23). What comes through in these references is that an interpreter was repeatedly treated as an inferior subordinate whose name, just like that of a servant or a bodyguard, remains, at least in this particular case, unknown. In fact, it is unclear from the text of the report whether this interpreter was Noorian or someone else. This anonymity is particularly interesting here because, as later sources demonstrate, Dr Ward and Noorian not only got along very well but also became close friends; and the former was instrumental in bringing Noorian to America (Peters 1898: 4), where he became a successful dealer in antiquities. It was also through Ward's recommendation that Daniel Z. Noorian was hired as an interpreter and director of the workmen of the Babylonian Expedition to Nippur under the auspices of the University of Pennsylvania in 1888–90. On the other hand, in William H. Ward's unpublished diary, Noorian's name recurs quite frequently. This discrepancy between the official published reports and an unofficial diary perhaps reflects general attitudes towards interpreters and their mostly marginal place in the social and academic 'food chain'.

Ward's diary, a large excerpt of which had been published by Peters (1898), is a fascinating travelogue describing the natural landscapes, archaeological, historical, and religious monuments and sites, people and their customs, as well as occasional adventures of the expedition members. Noorian, who at the time was only 19 years old, emerges as capable and enterprising negotiator and assistant. There seems to have been a good deal of interaction between the locals – Arabs involved in archaeological digs, sheikhs, numerous guides – and the expedition members, and it is clear that in many cases these communications were only possible through Noorian's linguistic and cultural mediation. As can be seen from Ward's diary, Noorian's job went far beyond that of an interpreter and mediator: he was a bodyguard, accompanying Ward everywhere – especially on his short side-trips (Ward 1898: 328, 331, 335, 351, 353, 358, 359, 366), explorer, assistant photographer, Ward's constant companion, manager; he was responsible for hiring horses and boats, looking for accommodation for the team. As someone with first-hand knowledge of the intricate multi-ethnic situation in the region, he understood very well how to appeal to the representatives of different confessions and of different ethnic backgrounds (Ward 1898: 337, 342, 343, 344, 346).

As it emerges from Dr Ward's notes, travelling throughout the Near East was not for the timid. One day, on the way to Niffer (Nippur), the caravan of the Wolfe Expedition unexpectedly encountered a group of 'mysterious horsemen,' fifteen in number, armed with guns and waving about some sort of banner – 'a red kerchief on a spear'. They turned out to be the Affech Arabs, who left their flocks to make sure that the caravan did not belong to their enemies of the el-Baij tribe:

> As we approached, they first concealed themselves behind bushes and thorns, and were ready to shoot from a safe place. Noorian and the guide went ahead, and our *zaptieh* in the rear. The guide waved his *meshlah* and made signs that we were friends. They were as ready for peace as we were, and began to march and sing, as well as we could make out:

> > Ya Beg, eshha bina medani
> > Ya Beg, eshha bina el nesrani

Which would mean:

> > O Beg, we long for the field of battle,
> > O Beg, we long to meet the Christians.

But it was not very easy to catch the words, and our guide, when asked, said that they were singing:

> > O Beg, we are beating out nitre.

> That is, to make powder for war. We stayed with them but a few minutes, and were glad to escape so peaceably, even though the song was not reassuring. We left them marching and shouting. (Ward 1898: 325–6)

Similar encounters followed suit: while spending a night not far from Bismya, the team had to put up a tent next to those of the Beni Rechab Arabs:

> who had just come from the Tigris. … Our soldier told them that we had been sent by the Government to see what could be done to control the irrigation of the country and make it productive. At night, after sitting and talking, the Arabs danced about wildly, singing war-songs, and after we had retired we heard guns fired, and bullets passed near our tent. When we asked if they wished to frighten us, they replied that it was to frighten wild beasts and robbers. (Ward 1898: 328)

In the course of their journey, the Wolfe Expedition encountered and had to interact with many groups and individuals, whose attitude ranged from neutral, to curious, from friendly, to plain hostile. One day at Shatra, it was:

> a busy day at our rooms at the khan, receiving visitors. The captain came early … and stayed, and talked freely in Turkish about Turkey and the Government,

and his longing to go to America and study machinery ... and railroads. (Ward 1898: 336)

Later on:

an Armenian doctor came and talked a long while about politics, speaking Armenian, so that others might not understand. He asked all sorts of questions about Egypt, the French in southern China, the Congo Conference, the opinion of people about Turkey, and what would be likely upshot when war came, – whether a partition or protectorate of Turkey. Although wearing the Turkish uniform, he has no love for Turkish rule. He does not want a Russian protectorate or rule, but wants English railroads, and an Armenian autonomy, like the Bulgarian. (Ward 1898: 336)

Hidden tensions and open conflicts between the Arab clans, Turks and Arabs, Christians and Muslims, and everyone in between, at times involved the expedition and its members – directly or indirectly, and had to be dealt with:

During the day and evening all the other officers in the command [all Turks] called. They all feel like exiles from Constantinople, and despise the ignorant, uncultivated Arabs, who eat their pilaf with their fingers, rolling it into ball and tossing it into their mouths. They say the Arabs hate them and look at upon them as *Kafirs*, and they repay hate and abuse for hate. (Ward 1898: 337)

We sent out for coffee, and the *kafejee* refused to send cups for a Christian. Our captain [a Turk] happened to hear him, and he cursed the man, his father, mother, brother, sisters, and all his relations. (Ward 1898: 338)

Our Arab guide would not eat our food, and our soldier [Turkish], Abbas, whom we had brought all the way from Hillah, abused him generally, saying that he could not eat good bulghur with butter, but would wait for bad bulghur without butter made by Arabs. (Ward 1898, 347)

While at Ramadieh, the expedition witnessed the following scene:

In front of the coffee-room there was a crowd and a fight. The man attacked was thrown down, and cried out convulsively to Noorian for help, saying that he would be a Christian if Noorian would help him, that the Christians have more mercy than Moslems. Noorian had a whip in his hand and he went to the man's help, talking only in Turkish, as if he were an officer, and threatening to put the man in prison who made the attack, and who was actually trying to kill his victim with a knife. And yet the two were brothers-in-law.

The man got up bleeding, but we did not hear of his becoming a Christian.
(Ward 1898: 357)

Noorian, having been raised trilingual (he spoke Armenian, Turkish and
Arabic), was a perfect mediator and guide, helping Ward and his team
navigate the uncertain, turbulent, and often treacherous waters of the multi-
cultural Ottoman empire.

The Wolfe Expedition was the main incentive for yet another American
archaeological venture – the Babylonian Expedition, under the auspices of the
University of Pennsylvania, was sent out to excavate the ancient Nippur.

The Babylonian Expedition of the University of Pennsylvania 1888–90: First and Second Campaigns

Nippur was one of several sites singled out and recommended for future exploration by the Wolfe expedition (Peters 1898: 31). An American expedition
affiliated with the University of Pennsylvania carried out work at Nippur in
four campaigns, from 1888 to 1900. Incomplete accounts of this work have
been published by John Punnett Peters and Hermann V. Hilprecht (Peters
1897; 1898; Hilprecht 1903) and they remain the main published source
of information about the first two archaeological campaigns (1888–9 and
1889–90), in the course of which Daniel Z. Noorian was employed as interpreter and director of the workmen. We are particularly concerned here
not with historical reality *per se* but rather with the activities and image of
Noorian as described by Peters and Hilprecht, for that reflected their attitude
towards their employee – a native on whom they greatly depended for much
of their official and unofficial communication while in the field.

Once the 'The Babylonian Exploration Fund' was called into existence and
a significant amount of the necessary funds was secured, Dr John Punnett
Peters, at the time a professor of Old Testament languages and literature at
the Episcopal Divinity School in Philadelphia and Professor of Hebrew at
the University of Pennsylvania, was confirmed as director of the Philadelphia
Babylonian Expedition. John D. Prince served as his secretary. Other members
included Hermann V. Hilprecht and Robert Francis Harper, Assyriologists;

John H. Haynes, business manager, commissary, and photographer; Percy Hastings Field, an architect. Actual excavations took place from 6 February to 15 April 1889 (Hilprecht 1903: 300).

The second campaign took place from 14 January to 3 May 1890. J. P. Peters remained director, although this time he was joined only by J. H. Haynes (Hilprecht 1903: 320). Daniel Z. Noorian, the interpreter of the Wolfe Expedition, who since 1885 had been residing in America, was invited to join the expedition during the first two campaigns (Hilprecht 1903: 299–300; Peters 1898: 4). 'He was engaged on a salary, as originally proposed, as an interpreter, and, after excavations should commence, director of the workmen' (Peters 1898: 10).

Although negotiations with Constantinople regarding the *firman* had begun well in advance, it was uncertain whether the Americans would actually get permission to excavate. Therefore, only three members of the team; the director Dr John Peters, Dr Harper and Mr. Prince sailed to Constantinople in June 1888. Noorian and Dr Hilprecht were to follow them later (Peters 1898: 11). Thus, for several months Dr Peters had to rely on his two members and random interpreters to help him communicate with the local authorities.

Here is how Dr Peters describes their arrival into the harbour of the Golden Horn one early morning:

> We were surrounded by a host of small boats, and invaded by porters and hotel runners speaking every conceivable language horribly. ... We were rescued from their clutches by the appearance on the scene of the *cawass* of our legation, resplendent in gold embroidery, and armed with a sabre and some immense old-fashioned horse pistols. Prince (member of the team), who could speak all sorts of out-of-way languages, like Turkish, Gypsy, Bohemian, and Danish, was able to enter into communication with him, and inform him that we were the persons he had been sent to bring on shore. (Peters 1898: 22)

Having settled in Constantinople, Dr Peters had to pay visits to the officials, in order to facilitate the issue of *firman*. His reports contain interesting observations about the linguistic abilities of the local authorities. 'Mr. Pendleton King, Chargé d'Affaires, Mr. A. A. Gargiulio, the wise and wily Dragoman' and Dr Peters went to visit the Grand Vizier, Kiamil Pasha. 'He was cautious, but friendly, at least in manner. We conversed in English, drank Turkish coffee, and smoked cigarettes' (Peters 1898: 22). It seems that, in this case, the presence of the Mr Gargiulio the Dragoman was not needed for interpreting *per se*, as the Kiamil Pasha 'spoke English excellently' (Peters 1898: 23). On the other hand, the Minister of Public Instruction, Munif Pasha, was not fluent in English at all:

> [Having] studied a little in Germany, [he] spoke French and German, both imperfectly, and a few words of English. ... He did not receive us at first in a friendly manner. ... A long discussion ensued. Finally Gargiulio went over and whispered in his ear, after which he became somewhat more friendly, ... and said that ... he would see me again the following Tuesday. (Peters 1898: 23)

In addition to interpreting, 'the wise and wily' Mr Gargiulio acted here as a suave and persuasive mediator. Mr Neshaka, the American consular agent, who simultaneously worked as interpreter at the British Consulate, also rendered his services to Peters (Peters 1897: 17).

Peters himself claimed to have been barely able to speak Turkish. Nevertheless, when a *zaptieh* asked him once about America and whether Americans had a sultan, he was able to explain to him, with his 'poor Turkish, and with the aid of ... fingers' the system of electing a president every four years. The *zaptieh* was greatly impressed and was later seen conveying this information to other Arabs (Peters 1898: 224). Later on, while attempting to get a *zaptieh* escort for his travels from Damascus to Palmyra, Dr Peters had an unpleasant encounter with a Governor-General in Damascus. This story provides another interesting sketch of the language policies of the Ottomans and Peters' own ability to speak Turkish. That Governor-General:

> although governor of an Arab-speaking region, ... was unable to speak one word of Arabic. The Turks treat the Arabs as conquered race, and put over them not infrequently men like this man, Ahmed Pasha, as completely a foreigner to them as a Russian would be to us. He was, moreover, notoriously corrupt. As he could not speak Arabic, Mr. Syufi [Director of the Imperial Ottoman Bank] was unable to interpret for me, and the official interpreter of the *vilayet* was sent for. I preferred, however, to speak directly to the Governor-General in such poor Turkish as I could muster. (Peters 1897: 21–2)

Once the digging was in full swing, Peters had to communicate with the Arab-speaking workers and their chiefs when Noorian the interpreter had been sent away on business. Apparently, Peters managed to use effectively his 'scant supply of Arabic" (Peters 1897: 77, 79), which he regularly perfected. While in Nippur, Peters received instructions in Arabic from a son of local *mullah* (Peters 1897: 92). He was also making some progress in Turkish, and, during the second campaign, he dictated to a commissioner, 'by the help either of Noorian or the Turkish dictionary, the memoranda' for his reports and letters to the museum (Peters 1897: 92).

When the permission to excavate had been obtained, Daniel Z. Noorian arrived in Alexandria where he was supposed to meet Dr Peters and the rest of the team. Noorian's local connections, knowledge of indigenous character and what one might call savviness, were required right away:

> The custom-house authorities at Alexandretta were suspicious of foreigners and especially of Americans who have been accused of smuggling arms and other contraband articles into the country. ... It was only the shrewdness of Noorian that saved from seizure the part of our rifles ... Noorian smuggled the rifles on the shore at night by wrapping them into rubber and submerging them into the water on the shady side of the boat – so the when the authorities arrived it simply looked as if a man was taking a row in the moonlight. (Peters 1898: 70)

Noorian's brother Jeremiah proved useful as well, having helped Daniel carry the guns on his back to Beylan, where they were handed over to Haynes (Peters 1898: 71) and subsequently made their way to the expedition camp.

Once Noorian joined the team, his duties immediately turned out to be much more varied than those of an interpreter and director of workmen. Just like with William H. Ward of the Wolfe Expedition, Noorian often gave Peters advice on local customs, behaviour and rules of hospitality. For example, when the head of a village, an old man, having provided the expedition members with an uninhabited house to spend a night in, came to visit and 'set a dish of curdled goat's milk before' them, it was Noorian who explained to Peters that it was his 'duty to accept, eat with much relish and pay for.' Peters lamented: 'this was the first of a long series of sacrifices of my palate and digestion to the demands of hospitality and politeness which I was set to make' (Peters 1898: 75).

When the members of the expedition travelled around, Noorian often arranged for the armed escorts (*zaptieh*), and was often dispatched with *zaptieh* to secure rooms and accommodation (Peters 1898: 115). He was also known to have taken issues of discipline in his own hands – and once took on 'the responsibility to flog a muleteer who disobeys' (Peters 1898: 87). When asked to, he copied and translated Arabic inscriptions (Peters 1898: 93) encountered during travel and took photographs if needed. In addition to translating official documents and letters, Noorian seems to have been in charge of many basic but quite necessary errands, such as engaging boats, rearing gazelles (for meat), eavesdropping. By and large, he was on constant lookout, hunting for information, listening to what was happening in and around the camp and informing Peters about the general goings on. Something he overheard once made the team members suspicious of the antiquities that a Syrian Catholic priest at Deir was trying to sell to them. After a closer look, they all turned out to be forgeries (Peters 1898: 117). On more than one occasion, armed with a Winchester, Noorian acted as bodyguard when the team travelled around (Peters 1897: 270), and tended to the wounds of, and accompanied, sick members of the team to Baghdad (Peters 1897: 48, 73, 77).

Although Peters had a rather rudimentary knowledge of Turkish and Arabic, he could manage a basic conversation. Nonetheless, he required Noorian to interpret for him. Not only was this much more convenient for Peters, but the presence and participation of an interpreter helped to create a certain distance between the conversing parties, and added 'official' tone to a dialogue. Conversing though an interpreter is one of the oldest practices in the history of diplomacy and Peters often exploited it. Mekota, one of the sheikhs of the Affech tribe living in the vicinity of the expedition camp in Nippur, had his eye on Peters' gun. After his repeated demands had been politely ignored, he decided to proceed with his request through a frontman. His scribe, having found out that Peters could manage some written Arabic, wrote a note suggesting that Mekota wanted his pistol, and handed the note to the director. Incidentally, the government soldier who stood on guard by the door 'became very nervous and tried to tell … [Peters] something in Turkish,' as he did not want the Arabs and the Americans conversing and striking deals without the governmental representatives knowing what was going on. Moreover, the guard probably did not understand Arabic. Peters, pretending that he did not understand the text, sent for Noorian. When the latter arrived, he was not asked to translate the text for Peters, but was asked to convey to the scribe that the director did not understand Arabic now, 'but hoped to do so next year' (Peters 1898: 282), thus indefinitely postponing both the conversation and the gifting of the gun.

In his published reports, Peters repeatedly praises Noorian for his talent and efficiency in dealing with the workmen: 'In the matter of dealing with Arabs' he 'was compelled to trust entirely to the experience of Noorian' (Peters 1898: 94, 236). Indeed, as director of workmen, Noorian was responsible for selecting and engaging the men from among the local tribes; most importantly, however, he had to organize, direct and generally manipulate them, making sure that they would do the required work properly. According to Peters, most of these men were 'notorious antiquity thieves.' Noorian thought that he could exercise some control by selecting workmen from two rival villages 'in the hope of preventing fraud or collision, by means of rivalry and mutual distrust' (Peters 1898: 212, 221). This did not always work out the way he thought or hoped it would. An interesting yet disturbing incident illustrates well Noorian's relationship with Dr Peters, his attitude towards the Arabs and the generally dangerous conditions for archaeologists in the 'Bible Lands' in the late 1880s. When the expedition arrived at Nippur and was settling on a hill that belonged to no-one, an Arabic tribe, el-Hamza, volunteered to help. Soon, members of a rival tribe, el-Behahtha, showed up, claiming that the site of ancient Nippur was within their territory and it was they who had to 'take care' of the expedition – naturally, for compensation. After exchanging sharp words, both parties began a menacing war dance and chanting. Peters decided to interfere, with the intention of turning this serious incident into a joke, 'and called Noorian to go ... [with him] and interpret.' Noorian, having understood what the tribesmen were actually saying, refused at first, so Peters decided to go on his own. Noorian, 'who was anything but a coward' joined Peters and decided to play along:

[He] entered into the spirit of the matter admirably, and interpreted my little jokes far better than I made them, so that soon the whole party of us were roaring with laughter, and we were successfully driving the Arabs down the hill. (Peters 1898: 240)

However, several days later a war did break out between the two tribes and several men were killed (Peters 1898: 239–41).

At the end of the first campaign, the expedition camp was burned down by a group of Arabs who were particularly disappointed by the outcome of what

they regarded as their business dealings with the Americans. The team had
to leave immediately and soon reached Baghdad. On the way there, Harper
handed in his resignation. Haynes said he would resign:

> Noorian, who knew better than any of us the feeling of the Arabs, handed me
> a written statement to the effect that he would under no circumstances return
> to Nippur, as he believed that his life would be endangered by doing so. (Peters
> 1898: 288)

According to John P. Peters:

> [their] first year at Nippur had ended in failure and disaster. I had failed to win
> the confidence of my comrades. None of them agreed with me in my belief
> in the importance of Nippur, and the desirability of excavating down to the
> foundations. The Arabs had proved treacherous. The Turkish authorities disbe-
> lieved our story of Arab treachery, and suspected us of plotting with our Turkish
> commissioner to carry away antiquities. (Peters 1898: 288)

Still, Peters was almost confident that, having had time to think things over,
Noorian would be willing to come back to Nippur with him (Peters 1898:
289). The director was correct, and Noorian soon did change his mind and
assured Peters that he would return for the second campaign (Peters 1897:
15, 47).

Unfortunately, the general state of affairs had not changed during the
second campaign, as the workmen:

> maintained their attitude of hostility, and on one occasion their quarrel came
> to blows. Several times quarrels took place between individuals in the trenches,
> and more than once Noorian or I prevented bloodshed only by throwing
> ourselves on the assailants, separating them, and confiscating their arms. (Peters
> 1897: 86)

Under the circumstances, Noorian often had to assume the role of an
informer, listening to the Arab workmen talking among themselves, and
passing information on to Peters. Once, Noorian lay awake by the fire unable
to sleep because of a toothache and heard the Arabs discussing the equipment
of the expedition (Peters 1897: 57). Having detected an unhealthy interest he
informed Peters and the theft was prevented. Learning accidentally that Arabs
ascribed magical powers to the members of the expedition proved very useful.

Peters and Noorian decided to capitalize on this knowledge and one day, after a donkey was stolen and the culprit refused to confess, they organized a small but quite spectacular fireworks display in the middle of the night. As they initially promised that all goods stolen from them or from their men would bring a curse on the guilty, the fireworks were taken by the Arabs as a sign of their magical ability and mysterious powers to make stars fall from heaven. This had the desired effect and 'the pilfering ... stopped forthwith' (Peters 1897: 68–9; see also Hilprecht 1903: 323–5, for a not-so-enthusiastic description of this story).

Noorian was routinely involved in everyday dealings with mostly unwanted visitors (for example, Arabs performing a war-dance and screaming 'Down with the Christians!'), at times physically pushing them away from the camp (Peters 1898: 244). Some (if not most) of Noorian's duties might be best described as 'public relations' – mediation between the Americans and the workmen, and various representatives of the neighbouring Arab tribes, who constantly visited the camp and asked for money or guns, and occasionally threatened the expedition (Peters 1897: 66, 67, 82). At times, Noorian was personally subjected to direct danger:

> Berdi [one of the Arab chiefs] threatened to burn us down and murder Noorian, because we had not taken all our men from him, and because we had not paid him a salary for the men we had taken. ... Berdi murdered two of his brothers in their sleep, and is believed to be capable of anything. (Peters 1898: 254)

Throughout Peters' reports, Noorian is constantly credited with having figured out the right approach to the workmen at Nippur. He even claims that, eventually, they became much more effective than in the beginning (Peters 1897: 111–12). Apparently, Noorian was able to achieve this 'by keeping them constantly in good humor, and under vigilant surveillance, stimulating them by competition, and awakening their interest by explaining what things meant and what they were doing' (Peters 1897: 94). Noorian would spend every 'morning in the trenches, examining and directing' (Peters 1897: 89). If the job was not being done satisfactorily, the crafty interpreter-cum-supervisor had additional means to influence the workmen:

> Noorian stationed himself in the trenches with a light chain in his hands and when interest flagged and the processions of basket-carriers moved slowly and

> listlessly, he would stand at the outlet, swing his chain in his hands, and bring
> it down on the back of him whoever lagged, at the same time cheering them on
> to greater exertions, sometimes by ridicule sometimes by jest and merriment,
> It looked like the old days when Nippur was built. ... Only Noorian's whip was
> not so used as to do any injury. It was a pretense rather than a reality, but a very
> effective pretense. (Peters 1897: 95)

On the other hand, maintaining a position of a just man who looks out for
his employees, Noorian once violently assaulted a *zaptieh* who accused one
of the best workmen of the expedition of killing his wife, 'indignant at such
treatment of an unconvicted prisoner' (Peters 1897: 86). Noorian was almost
always present when Peters communicated with the workmen; in order to
foster closer relationships, he would spend some time with them after work,
sitting with them by the fire at night and encouraging the sheikh to tell stories
(Peters 1897: 56). He also used to read the Koran with Obeid, son of a local
mullah (Peters 1897: 92).

Towards the end of the second campaign Daniel Z. Noorian definitely
became more of a companion to Peters, who consulted him on many issues
and often took his advice (Peters 1898: 248). When the campaign was over,
Peters and Noorian decided to do some travelling before returning home.
They visited Mecca:

> the most sacred spot of the Moslem world. I [Peters] expected to find a city so
> fanatical toward strangers that I could not traverse the streets without an escort.
> Such were the conditions ... forty years before ..., but all has changed since
> then. Although Christians may now live in the city, yet hatred of the Turks has
> at least helped to make people look with favor on the 'Franks,' for the latter both
> the Persians and the Arabs of Irak see as their only hope of deliverance from the
> Ottoman yoke. I could wander through the city at will, and only the mosque was
> forbidden ground. (Peters 1897: 322)

During these travels, Daniel Noorian continued to act as an interpreter and
guide. On the other hand, he occasionally found himself in a role of a tourist,
while visiting the sacred places of Islam – a risky endeavour for a non-Muslim.
Having first-hand knowledge of the Arab and Turkish cultural traditions,
Noorian, accompanied by a Muslim guide, decided to undertake something
that would be extremely dangerous for any foreigner. While in Nejef, he
managed to visit the Meshed Ali and then describe to Peters what he saw in

great detail. Noorian and Artin (another Armenian who accompanied them during part of their trip):

> although Christians and Armenians, were smuggled into the sacred precincts by our Arabs, the latter as Persian, the former as a Turk from Stamboul. Noorian reported that at the entrance they made him kiss the chain across the gate, and both the doorposts. Then he entered the court, which was surrounded by alcove-like rooms, open in front, such as one finds all the great khans on the Persian pilgrim routes. (Peters 1897: 322)

Following a description of the interior and a story about how Noorian was made to repeat three or four prayers, Peters provides a rather sarcastic footnote that adds a particularly cynical tone to this unusual visit:

> It should be said that the Imam who escorted Noorian was also a priest of Ishtar, and in the intervals between prayers was offering, for a suitable consideration, to provide him with a woman. (Peters 1897: 323n1)

Understandably:

> Noorian was too nervous to notice things as fully as he wished, and our men also were nervous and hurried him. He proposed making another visit, but the following day a Baghdad merchant recognized him on the street, and after that the risk was too great, for if he had been detected he would surely have been killed. However, he accomplished the rare feat of penetrating and exploring this famous mosque. (Peters 1897: 322–4)

At Kerbela, Noorian and Abbas visited Meshad Husein (Husein's mosque). Apparently, 'he spent more time in this than in Meshed Ali, ... for Abbas ..., who had unexpectedly become pious since our visit to Nejef, fell praying tediously, and, in order not to betray himself, Noorian was obliged to imitate all his motions' (Peters 1897: 330).

From the published accounts of Peters and Hilprecht, it becomes apparent that Noorian played a rather significant role during the first two campaigns of the Babylonian Expedition of the University of Pennsylvania. Interestingly enough, in the derivative discussions of the Nippur excavation by the University of Pennsylvania, albeit based on Peters and Hilprecht, Daniel Z. Noorian once again becomes virtually invisible and is either not mentioned at all or very much in passing (see, for example, Rogers 1900; Meade 1974: 51, 53, 57; Fagan 1979; Kuklick 1996).

At the end of the second campaign in Nippur, Noorian's contract ended, and, having visited his home in Sert, he returned to the United States 'to put the experience acquired in two expeditions to practical use, as a dealer in antiquities' (Peters 1897: 343). Probably, the idea of such a career had been planted in Noorian's head when he moved to the US in 1885, after the Wolfe Expedition – if not earlier, by William H. Ward himself. While travelling with the Babylonian expedition, Noorian often used his time in various cities they visited or passed through to meet up with various dealers, to sample their offerings and to acquire objects as well – both on behalf of the members of the expedition and American institutions, and 'to replenish his own stocks' (Peters 1898: 222–3). He also undertook short reconnaissance trips to 'hunt up antiquities and information,' to collect stamped bricks and bits of pottery (Peters 1898: 199, 213), and undoubtedly to build up his own network of dealers that would ensure his continuous supply of the antiquities. The life and work of Noorian in America is addressed in the next chapter.

5

Daniel Z. Noorian: the 'Afterlife' of an Interpreter

Throughout his mature life Daniel Noorian, an interpreter for the Wolfe Expedition and for the two Babylonian Campaigns of the University of Pennsylvania, probably did not associate himself with this profession. However, ultimately he did belong to a large faction of dragomans who, in Egypt and the Near East, facilitated communication between the natives and the visitors, i.e. provided interaction, however superficial, between East and West. Many of these dragomans will remain forever invisible and unknown, while for some a name on a calling card will be all that is left of them (Figure 10). It was perhaps due to his collaboration with the American teams of archaeologists in Babylonia and Nippur that Noorian was able to move to the USA, where, with the help of available records, we are able to follow him into his post-interpreter 'afterlife' as an art dealer.

Daniel Zado Noorian, this interpreter-turned-quite-successful antiquities dealer, died at his home in Newark, New Jersey, on the evening of 10 January 1929. He was 64 years old. His unpretentious and tasteful tombstone in the Rosedale Cemetery in Montclair, New Jersey, has no mention of his memorable career as interpreter. A brief epitaph, flanked by two stylized Mesopotamian trees of life, simply reads: 'Daniel Z. Noorian. Archaeologist. Explorer. Art collector' (Figure 11).

Despite the omission of his short-lived stint as interpreter, this job was instrumental in launching and expanding his career in America. It was through the appointment with the Wolfe Expedition that he was able to establish connections that eventually secured his future. We do not know how Reverend William H. Ward, the director of the Wolfe Expedition, and

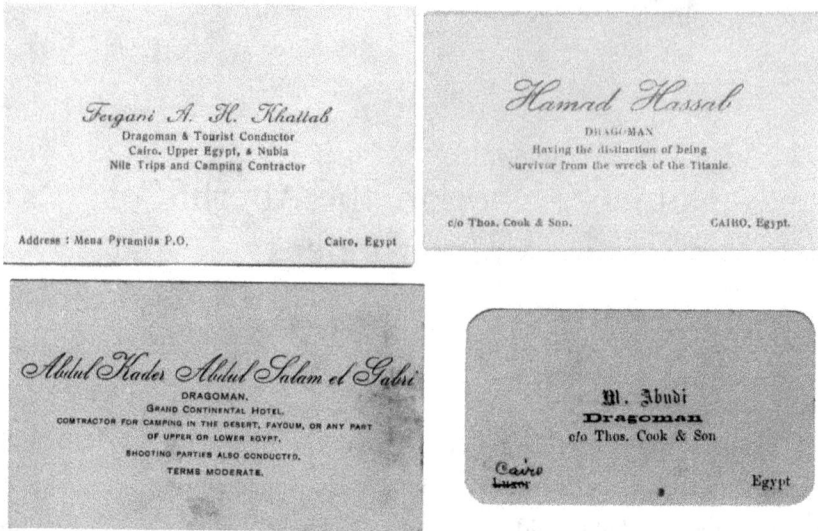

Figure 10: Dragoman business cards, of various dates. Top right: Hassab, Hamad. Calling card (Cairo, Egypt). Brooklyn Museum Libraries. Wilbour Library of Egyptology. Special Collections.

Daniel Z. Noorian, a 19-year-old native of Sert, met in Constantinople. When the expedition came to the end, Noorian followed Rev Ward to America. On his passport application from 1899, Noorian claims to have first entered the United States in August 1885 on board the SS *Waesland*. Indeed, *Waesland* did arrive at New York from Antwerp on 6 August 1885. According to the immigration statistics, the vessel contained 338 passengers altogether. Although Noorian's name is not to be found on the *Waesland*'s passenger list, it has to be pointed out that several of its passengers remained unlisted and were simply added as digits.

Based on indirect evidence, it can be assumed that upon his arrival young Daniel stayed with Rev Ward and his family in Newark, New Jersey. It also must have been under his guidance that Noorian enrolled in Rutgers Preparatory School in New Brunswick, New Jersey. Established in 1766, it was the oldest preparatory school in the state; it was a boarding school at the time Noorian attended. He graduated in 1888, just before going back to Nippur with the University of Pennsylvania expedition.

Figure 11: Gravestone of Daniel Z. Noorian and Belle Ward Noorian, Rosedale Cemetery, Montclair, Essex County, New Jersey, USA.

It was on account of this upcoming adventure, and probably also because William H. Ward, as the editor of the *Independent*, had connections in the world of published news, that Noorian's name appears prominently in local and national newspapers. The *Chicago Daily Tribune*; *Morning Oregonian* (Portland, Oregon); *New Berne Weekly Journal*; *San Francisco Chronicle*; the *Daily Journal* (New Berne, North Carolina), among others, all reprint (with negligible variations) essentially the same article with rather dramatic titles: 'To Dig Up Babylon', 'Babylon to be Resurrected: The Last of the Party to Dig

the Ruins About to Leave'; 'Babylon's Ruins: The Expedition Which Proposes
to Explore Them'; 'To Explore Babylon'; 'To Explore Babylon: The Ruins of the
Ancient City to be Dug Up by Americans'. The *Daily Journal* provides a playful
preface: 'Outside of the manufacturing of trunks and jewellery one does not
usually hear very much about Newark, N.J.; but the city has been coming to
the front in another way during these past few days' (*Daily Journal* 1888: 2).
And then it continues:

> Daniel Z. Noorian of Newark, N.J., will be the important man in the party that is
> going to dig up the ruins of ancient Babylon next winter. It is a mighty important
> expedition, although there has been no blow made about it. It will be the first
> party consisting almost entirely of Americans that ever set out determined to
> thoroughly explore one of the great buried cities of old. Mr. Noorian is about the
> only member of the expedition who is not American. He is Armenian by birth
> and education. He came to this country some years ago, and has resided with
> Dr. William Hayes Ward, editor of the New York *Independent*, who is himself an
> explorer. Noorian goes as the interpreter of the party. He will also superintend the
> work of digging up the ruins of Babylon … . Noorian will leave in the middle of
> August, and will join the party at Alexandretta, where the journey on horseback
> will commence. … A large quantity of provisions will be taken along, and each
> member of the party will be armed to protect themselves against the wild beasts
> and brigands. Arabs will be employed at 10 to 20 cents per day to do the excavating,
> and several hundred will be put to work. Picks, shovels, and wheelbarrows are to
> be taken along. … The expense of the present expedition will be defrayed by the
> Babylon exploration fund, subscribed by Philadelphians. … The territory between
> the Tigris and the Euphrates, in Mesopotamia, abounds in buried cities, most of
> which are of Biblical interest. Nearly 100 have been discovered. Explorations will
> be made by the present party in entirely new places and some important discov-
> eries in archaeological interest are looked for. (*Daily Journal* 1888: 2)

When Noorian returned to America from Nippur in 1890, in October of that
year he became a naturalized American citizen, and continued to reside with
Rev Ward and his two sisters on Abington Avenue in Newark. On his passport
application of 1899, Hetta L. H. Ward, the Rev Ward's unmarried 'artist' sister,
signs as a witness. It seems that Noorian developed an attachment to this
neighbourhood, as several years later he bought himself a house on the same
street – at 60 Abington Avenue. He was to reside in that house for the rest of
his life.

It is not known how Daniel Noorian became interested in the antiquities business or who suggested to him that this occupation would be a lucrative one. Perhaps it was Dr Ward, who during his sojourn in Babylonia in 1884–5 was thinking of ways to build up American collections of Near Eastern antiquities in general and of cuneiform tablets in particular. Already, in the first reports of the Wolfe Expedition, he was proclaiming: 'I hardly need do more than suggest how advantageous it would be for American scholarship if we might have in Baghdad a permanent resident who would make it his business to attend to our interests in archaeological matters' (Ward 1886: 33). Noorian, with the extensive network he was building up already in 1884–5, and again in 1888–90, was not living in Baghdad; even so, his activity as antiquities dealer at the time was undoubtedly seen by Rev Ward as highly advantageous for private and public collections in the USA.

By the time we first meet nineteen-year-old Noorian employed as interpreter by the Wolfe Expedition, he had already been engaged in collecting tablets and other objects, some of which he would sell on the spot, while the majority were eventually brought to America. From the beginning he seems to have had a good eye for beautiful and rare objects: for example, a fragment of a fifth century BC Attic red-figure rhyton, now at the Museum of Fine Arts (MFA) in Boston (acc. no. 26.15), was purchased by him 'in the early part of January 1885' in Babylon (Museum of Fine Arts Boston 2015). In addition to this fragment, the MFA acquisitions from Noorian dating from before 1894 included fragments of seventeeth century European fabric, Egyptian scarabs, Roman and Phoenician glass, and fragments of Roman lead coffins. Already by 1894 he had a business set up at the Antique Art Rooms at 11 Central Avenue in Newark. In fact, many American museums now have in their possession objects acquired – directly or indirectly – from Noorian.

In the summer of 1895 Daniel Z. Noorian managed to sell a large collection of cuneiform documents to the Columbia University Library. Between four and five hundred clay tablets ranging in size from 2 to 25 cm^2 were consigned to Noorian directly from Baghdad. The majority was said to have come from Telloh, probably from the excavations of M. E. de Sarzec, who, having excavated at that site since 1877, in 1894 came upon a large cache of cuneiform documents. This deposit is said to have contained up to 300,000 tablets and was believed to be the temple archives (Arnold 1896:

iii-iv); it was dispersed throughout European and American public and private collections.

In 1896 Noorian's name is mentioned in an article on 'Glass Treasures', describing the fine specimens of ancient glass brought to the US and collected by private collectors and museums; two pieces owned by Daniel are singled out for their rarity and beauty (*Brooklyn Daily Eagle* 1896: 24).

A rather unabashed advertisement in the *Brooklyn Daily Eagle* from 25 November 1900 advertises Noorian's business – 'Antiques – Gems – Rugs' and 'Ancient Iridescent Phoenician and Greco-Roman Glass', located at 28 East 20th Street in New York:

> I have the largest and best collection carried by any dealer in the world, also a large assortment of objects of artistic and archaeological value especially suitable for presentation, avoiding duplication. Oriental antique silver and gold jewelry. Italian and Spanish Laces, Brocades, Embroideries, Velvets and Vestments. (*Brooklyn Daily Eagle* 1900: 3)

It appears that by 1900 Noorian had moved his gallery/showroom to Manhattan, where it remained until his death. Noorian's letterhead (Figure 12) features an impressive list of the 'source' countries for the antiquities he offered for sale; rarity, and artistic beauty, as well as the archaeological and scholarly value of the objects he carries, are also eloquently albeit briefly emphasized.

Nine extant letters from Noorian to General Luigi Palma di Cesnola, director of the Metropolitan Museum of Art at the time, dating from 1896, 1899 and 1901, are very curious as they throw some light on the relationship

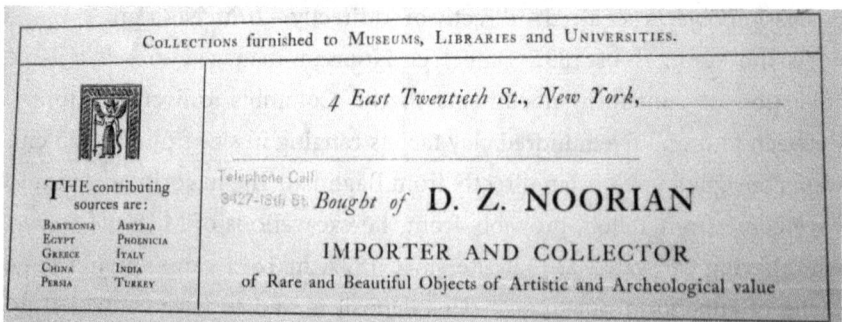

Figure 12: Letterhead of Daniel Z. Noorian.

between a dealer and a museum director, and elucidate some trick of the trade that an antiquities dealer might have used. Two additional letters from Reverend William H. Ward to General Cesnola (1897 and 1899)[1] demonstrate once again the close personal and probably professional ties shared by the former director of the Wolfe Expedition and Noorian. In his letters to Cesnola, Ward advocates for Noorian, and makes arrangements on his behalf. In Noorian's letters to Cesnola, Dr Ward's name is often mentioned, and his opinions are alluded to; moreover, Noorian offers several objects to the Museum 'at the request of Dr. Ward.' Apparently, William H. Ward knew Cesnola personally, as they had engaged in some business a few years previously. Although Ward did not personally purchase anything while in the Near East, on his way back he stopped in London and 'at his own expense' bought a collection of cuneiform documents, which he immediately offered to the Metropolitan Museum. In 1886, the Museum acquired Ward's collection of cuneiform tablets, thus becoming the first American museum to obtain such a sizable and important collection (Spar 1988: xiv).

In his letter from 27 January 1896, Noorian offered Cesnola 'a very large collection of Babylonian and Assyrian tablets unusual for the number of large and perfect tablets, as well as <u>cased</u> ones. Four fifths of the collection (which is about seven to eight hundred pieces) are <u>baked</u>.' Noorian claimed that the collection had been examined by several Assyriologists, in addition to Dr John P. Peters (the director of the University of Pennsylvania Expedition at Nippur) and Dr William Hayes Ward. Moreover, 'Dr. Ward has expressed a strong desire to see it secured in some way or another for the Metropolitan and it is at the recommendation of both that I write to call your attention to it.' 'When you see it, the Collection will speak for itself. I would like to praise it to you but I leave that to others who have seen it and I have no doubt both Dr. Ward and Dr. Peters would speak very highly of it, should you feel inclined to make inquiries of them.' The majority of these pieces were said to have come from the excavations of M de Sarzec in Telloh. A particularly large tablet, 'a foot square, the largest tablet known in this country and one of the largest found

---

[1]   All eleven letters are in the Office of the Secretary Records kept in the Archives of The Metropolitan Museum of Art, in the following folders: "Purchases – Authorized – Antiquities (Assyrian and Babylonian) – Noorian, 1896–1897, 1909" and "Purchases – Authorized – Antiquities (General) – Offered for sale by D. Z. Noorian 1899, some prob. Purchased, 1899, 1901". We are grateful to Jim Moske and Barbara File for permitting us to work with these letters and to use them in this study.

by M. de Sarzec,' was among them. The rest of the tablets came 'from different parts of Babylonia such as Babylon, Birs-Nimrod, Abu-Haba, Warka, Yokha, and Habel-Ibrahim.' Appealing to one's feelings of competitiveness while trying to make a sale should be considered a good strategy: Noorian is careful to point out that, as far as he knows, the Louvre has not yet received the large tablets, as all of them went to the Imperial Museum at Constantinople. The tablets from the 'Tello[h] Great find' kept coming into Noorian's hands. More than three years later, on 10 November 1899, he wrote to Cesnola yet again and offered 'some hundred and fifty case tablets almost all perfect', 'some of the largest' he had ever had in his possession. Once again, Noorian is quick to emphasize that the Metropolitan Museum is the first institution he is offering this group to, and that even in the Philadelphia collection there are no comparable objects. In another letter, from 31 January 1899, when discussing some objects Cesnola was interested in, Noorian states that he 'can furnish … things … cheaper than anyone else can' as 'the à la Noorians prices are not so high as compared with other peoples prices.'

In his article on the seal cylinders, Reverend Ward thanks Daniel Z. Noorian who, 'by his acquaintance with the customs of the Orient and his skilled aid in detecting forgeries, has given … [him] much valuable aid' (Ward 1910: iv). It appears that Noorian developed a keen eye for objects of questionable authenticity. On at least two occasions, in 1906 and 1909, the Metropolitan Museum of Art also used Noorian as a dealer with an impeccable memory, and as an expert in forgeries. A 'Memorandum: Ancient Jewelry in the Gold Room'[2] describes these two visits: Noorian was asked by Edward Robinson, an Assistant Director of the Metropolitan Museum at the time, to examine a collection of jewellery that was thought to have come 'from the countries east of the Mediterranean.' Among them, Noorian managed to recognize and identify many of the pieces, as they had gone through his hands; he also designated several objects as much later 'Turkish' works – and these were immediately transferred into the 'modern section' of the Museum; several he dismissed as forgeries.

---

[2] This document is in the Office of the Secretary Records kept in the Archives of The Metropolitan Museum of Art, in the following folder: 'Purchases – Authorized – Antiquities (Assyrian and Babylonian) – Noorian, 1896–1897, 1909'.

The Hilprecht-Peters Controversy

Starting in 1905, one of the greatest feuds in the world of Assyriology, commonly referred to as the Hilprecht-Peters controversy, took place. John P. Peters, the director of the Nippur Expedition during the first two seasons made several serious accusations against Hermann V. Hilprecht, his colleague, and professor at the University of Pennsylvania. The Board of Trustees of the university had to react and put together a committee that was to act as a 'Court of Inquiry.' Numerous written and oral statements by Peters against Hilprecht were condensed by the committee into three major charges: 'the charge of literary dishonesty'; 'the charge of improperly retaining property belonging to the University of Pennsylvania'; 'the charge that what was found at Nippur has not just claim to be called a Temple Library' (Hilprecht 1908: 267). Several committee meetings took place and numerous scholars were invited to contribute statements – either oral or written. In addition to several short accounts of the dispute, Hermann V. Hilprecht himself compiled and published a 350-page-long volume of letters, documents and notes from the trial, 'presented to the public by H.V. Hilprecht' (Hilprecht 1908). Eventually, the Committee failed to find straightforward and convincing evidence to support the charges that Hilprecht had retained some of the objects acquired for the University of Pennsylvania Museum (charge two). The question of the Temple Library at Nippur (charge three) remained a tricky one, as several scholars who suspected, and even accused, Hilprecht of academic dishonesty thought that a cache of tablets discovered during the fourth campaign at Nippur did, in fact, belong to a temple library (Meade 1974: 75). As for the first accusation, of literary dishonesty, that remained up in the air. Although Hilprecht never made explicit claims, a read through his *Explorations in Bible Lands* would suffice to indicate that he had a tendency to take credit for the work of the others, John Hanes in particular. After a much-prolonged back-and-forth, Hilprecht resigned from the University in 1911. His academic career came to a standstill and he died in 1925. It has been noted that this clash of scholarly and human egos and personalities had a curious side effect: it did bring unusually wide publicity to Assyriology, which in turn prompted higher sales of the books on the subject, those by Peters (1897; 1898) and Hilprecht (1903) in particular (Meade 1974: 75–6).

What was Noorian's role in all this rigmarole? His name was often brought up during meetings, as some of the tablets whose provenance was questioned and/or challenged were in fact obtained by him on the antiquities market, a fact he openly admitted when questioned during the trial. Of main interest to us here are some additional details of Noorian's activities in the Near East that emerged in the course of the 'trial'. During the first two campaigns, Noorian had already acted as dealer – purchasing tablets and other objects – on behalf of Peters, for the Expedition and for his own collection (Hilprecht 1908: 48). Interestingly, one collection compiled by Noorian in 1888–90 was eventually acquired by the University of Pennsylvania Museum (Hilprecht 1908: 55). Noorian also purchased objects on behalf of Hilprecht and acted as his 'agent in receiving [tablets] from the Arabs and shipping [them] to England and America, with other tablets previously bought for [him] in Babylonia' (Hilprecht 1908: 235).

During this makeshift trial, while defending himself by shifting blame, Hilprecht brought up a letter written to him by Reverend Ward:

> August 1, 1891.
>
> ... Daniel [Noorian] came back about the same time you did, and is now with us. Dr. Peters has reported some very unfavorable stories about Daniel, on the credit of Mr. Haynes, who received them from Mustafa chiefly. I am not ready to believe them. I tell you this as you may hear of them. I cannot see but Daniel has tried to do well. He seems the same kind, lovable, sturdy fellow he always was, and he sent his regards to you. I hope you can visit us before long and see him. ... Ever most sincerely yours, William Hayes Ward. (Hilprecht 1908: 263)

Hilprecht then continues:

> I remember distinctly the report that Mr. Noorian, while employed in the service of the expedition, had levied a special tax upon the poor Arabs, which they had to pay to him. These were the stories which Dr. Ward at that time spoke of, adding, 'on the credit of Mr. Haynes, who received them from Mustafa. I am not ready to believe them. I tell you this as you may hear of them'. (Hilprecht 1908: 263)

Hilprecht further states that these rumours were the reason why Noorian had not been invited back for the third and fourth campaigns (Hilprecht 1908: 263). Whether this was a true story, or whether Mustafa attempted to undermine Noorian's reputation, we shall probably never know. It is worth noting however that neither this 'incident' nor indeed any disapproval of Noorian's behaviour ever made it into the expedition accounts of Peters or Hilprecht. It is perhaps significant that this story emerged in the aftermath of Hilprecht's trial in his rather bitter publication.

As we have seen, Noorian had much experience as 'importer' and agent and undoubtedly was savvy and practical enough to handle unexpected surprises connected with importing archaeological objects to America. One amusing episode concerned with the importation issues and status of the cuneiform tablets was written up in the *New York Times* in a short note entitled, 'Stone Tablet a Manuscript: Appraiser Defines Status of Inscription from Assyrian Tomb':

> A problem in etymology and archaeology combined was solved by General Appraiser Charles P. McClelland yesterday when he defined the dutiable status of a marble tablet, taken from the tomb of an Assyrian King, and bearing an inscription carved 800 years before Christ. The tablet, which is broken into four pieces for ease in transportation, was imported by D. Z. Noorian of New York, admittedly as a commercial speculation. It was assessed by the Collector as a manufacture of limestone at 50 per cent., and the importer demanded free entry for it as a manuscript. Among the witnesses called was Prof. Prince the Chair of Semitic Languages at Columbia University, who declared the tablet was as much a manuscript as a papyrus would be. Mr. McClelland refers to the Ten Commandments, which were written on stone, and declares it cannot be gainsaid that these tablets of stone were manuscript. He also quotes from Webster's Dictionary, which defines writing as 'the act of forming letters and characters on paper, wood, stone, or other material,' and sustained Mr. Noorian's contention. (*New York Times* 1905: 14)

Unfortunately, the appalling and wicked practice of breaking objects into several fragments 'for ease in transportation' persisted throughout a good part of the twentieth century.

Occasional reconnaissance and acquisition trips to Europe were part of Daniel Noorian's routine as an art dealer. In his letter to Cesnola from 19 September 1899, written from Italy, he relates that he bought 'many … things of interest.' Among them, a fine steel shield of Lombardian workmanship, which incidentally 'has a well known history and it belonged to an old Italian family but now it has found its way into the market'.

Among Noorian's clients, there were some important collectors, such as John Graver Johnson of Philadelphia. In 1903 he bought from him what at the time was believed to be the front panel of an early Renaissance *cassone* (marriage chest). This object, now identified as a spalliera painting that would have decorated a bedchamber in a Florentine palace, dates from the 1480s and is attributed to Jacopo del Sellaio; it is now in the Philadelphia Museum of Art. The painting features a group of Sabine women with their children standing between the Sabine and Roman armies and pleading for peace. In 1903 this purchase even warranted a short note in the *New York Times*: 'Philadelphia's habit of getting the better of New York in art matters is becoming chronic'. It was called a 'particularly attractive work of art' 'strongly influenced by Botticelli' and 'attributed to Fillippino Lippi' or Sellaio (*New York Times* 1903: 8). It was acquired by Noorian, or by one of his agents on his behalf, at the Panciatichi sale in 1902 in Florence. The Panciatichi family, whose history can be traced back to the eleventh century, moved to Florence from Pistoia in 1352. Their collection of paintings was one of the most important in Florence (Horner and Horner 1873: 103–6). From the collection of the same family came a nineteenth century Persian Qajar silver gilt shield, now in the St. Louis Art Museum. Since the 1870s, the Panciatichi family was slowly selling off its collection – from paintings to Persian armour – and Noorian kept an eye on one of the better-known Florentine collections. Noorian's name also appears once in a while in the articles reporting important art sales within the United States: at the sale of an anonymous private collector in March 1922, he acquired a panel painting entitled *Angels Crowning the Virgin*, by Innocenzo da Imola, for $775 (*New York Times* 1922: 12).

Daniel Noorian worked with a vast variety of objects from different time periods and from divers geographical areas, and at the end of his life managed to amass a rather significant collection. The sale of his possessions took place in 1931 – almost two years after his death – through the Anderson Galleries Inc., in New York City. It lasted three days (three sessions, 12–14 March) and consisted of six hundred and forty-two objects. These included a great variety of glass items – from Egyptian, Syrio-Roman and Phoenician to Bohemian and Venetian; Egyptian and Near Eastern antiquities; Persian lacquer, minia-tures and illuminated manuscripts; ancient and medieval jewellery; damasks, brocades, cashmeres and a nice selection of Oriental rugs; Rakka, majolica and Chinese porcelains; items of arms and armour – European and Eastern; furniture; paintings. The most important item at the Noorian sale was a marble statue of the Youthful St John, attributed at the time to Jacopo Sansovino. Years after Noorian's death, this sculpture, now part of the collection of the National Gallery in Washington DC, created quite a stir when for a while it was thought to be the work of the young Michelangelo (McLain 1965). It is now attributed to another Florentine sculptor, Giovanni Francesco Susini.[3]

Finding a good photograph of Noorian has proved an impossible task. According to a description provided by the man himself, on his US passport application of 1899 (he was 34 at the time), Daniel Noorian stood 5 feet 9 inches tall. He had an oval face with a high forehead, aquiline nose, strong chin and straight mouth. Brown eyes and auburn hair, with an overall 'ruddy' complexion, completed the picture. We know a handful of facts about Noorian's immediate family. His younger brother, Jeremiah Zado Noorian, the one who helped carrying the guns to the expedition camp (Peters 1898: 71), followed Daniel to America. He arrived at New York on board the SS *Lord Clive* in December 1892. He was almost twenty-one years old at the time. An even younger brother, Elias, who was thirteen, accompanied him. On the list of passengers both brothers are listed as students, with 'Newark' as their final destination, coming to join 'brother Daniel.' Their nationality and last residence is identified as 'Turkey.' Jeremiah, who preferred to be called Zado Noorian, became a well-known jeweller who also dabbled in dealing in antiquities, especially rugs (Albee 1908; Noorian 1909). By 1920, Zado, then in his mid-forties, was listed as unmarried and shared a household with one Margaret Noorian, age 68. Apparently, the widowed mother of the Noorian brothers joined them in America (Year: *1920*; Census Place: *Manhattan Assembly District 10, New York, New York*; Roll: *T625_1203*; Page: *7B*; Enumeration District: *761*; Image: *818*.). The place of birth for both of them was designated as 'Armenia' and the 'mother tongue' as Armenian, as opposed to the US Census of 1910, when Daniel Noorian's birthplace and native language were recorded as Turkey/Turkish (Year: *1910*; Census Place: *Newark Ward 8, Essex, New Jersey*; Roll: *T624_878*; Page: *1B*; Enumeration

---

[3] National Gallery of Art, acc. no. 2005.109.1

District: *0066*; FHL microfilm: *1374891*.). Both Zado and Margaret were listed as able to read and write and both could speak English.

In the early 1900s (prior to 1913), Daniel Noorian married Belle Ward from a rather important family at the time residing in New Jersey. Belle was the daughter of Robert Ward of Melbourne, England. The latter was brought to the US as a child by his father, Henry Ward, who was one of the founders of the wholesale woollen firm French & Ward. Belle's brother, Holcombe Ward, was a prominent tennis player. The last name of Noorian's wife curiously matches that of William H. Ward, Noorian's adopted American father. However, there does not seem to be any apparent connection between the two Ward families.

A representative of a national minority, born and raised in the multi-lingual milieu of the Ottoman Empire, by the age of nineteen he spoke at least four languages: Armenian, Turkish, Arabic and English. Intelligent, ambitious, enterprising, Daniel Z. Noorian became indispensable as interpreter, caretaker and assistant to several American archaeologists. It seems though that right from the start he was contemplating another career – that of 'antiquarian,' 'merchant,' 'dealer in art.' As we have seen, his work as interpreter was not simply to translate but also to arrange, appease, moderate, negotiate, compromise and communicate or to facilitate communication. Fittingly, and perhaps unbeknownst to him, Noorian's career as an art and antiquities dealer seemed strangely parallel in many ways to his job as interpreter.

6

Solomon Negima: A Dragoman and his Clients

The Testimonial Book of Dragoman Solomon N. Negima

In July 1891, Mrs Ella L. Goodknight, of Piqua, Ohio, wrote the latest in a series of letters recounting her travels and impressions of life abroad to her hometown newspaper, the *Miami Helmet*. Mrs Goodknight had just taken a trip from Jerusalem to Jericho, the Dead Sea and the Jordan river. The party, she describes as follows:

> Our company now consisted of fourteen tourists, all Americans, save Lord Dalrymple, of Scotland, with Mr. Turnham from London, as our conductor, and Solomon Negema, a Syrian, as dragoman. As a necessary protection against the Bedawin Arabs we were obliged to have the Shiek of the Jordan to accompany us. (Goodknight 1891)

Solomon Negima would be another invisible, silent interpreter, were it not for the survival of a remarkable document: his own testimonial book, in which he collected letters from clients, photographs and other personal memoranda, about eighty documents in total (Figure 13: Testimonial Book). At least five members of Mrs Goodknight's company wrote letters of recommendation for their dragoman, which he collected and pasted into his book, to show to prospective clients. Lord Dalrymple's letter, written on the stationary of the Grand Hotel Dimitri, Damascus, is formal, to the point, and lacks even a signature:

> Lord Dalrymple begs to state that he travelled in the spring of 1891 through Palestine and Syria with Suleiman Nejima as his dragoman, and has much pleasure in stating that he found him most intelligent, obliging, and useful in every way, and can most strongly recommend him to all parties wishing to travel through the above mentioned districts. (Negima 1885–1933: SN37, 18

Figure 13: The Testimonial Book of Dragoman Solomon N. Negima. © Rachel Mairs.

April 1891 Figure 14: Letter from Lord Dalrymple. Solomon's name is spelled in different ways by different writers.)

Mrs Goodknight reports that one of their fellow travellers, the Rev A. A. Williams of Lynn, Massachusetts, cut a piece of stone from the place where the Good Samaritan was said to have performed his act of charity, which he intended to have made into a gavel to present to his Masonic lodge. (Mark Twain's companions in the Holy Land were also enthusiastic chippers and defacers of rocks and monuments; Twain 1869: *passim.*) Rev Williams travelled on in Solomon Negima's company for longer than Lord Dalrymple, and wrote him a testimonial from the New Hotel in Beirut eleven days later:

> This certifies that we have travelled through the Holy Land with Solomon Negima as our Dragoman & find him to be not only kind & obliging but well qualified to fill the place & to give instructions concerning the different places of interest.
>
> We most cheerfully commend him to all who contemplate such a tour & especially our American friends. (Negima 1885–1933: SN35, 29 April 1891)

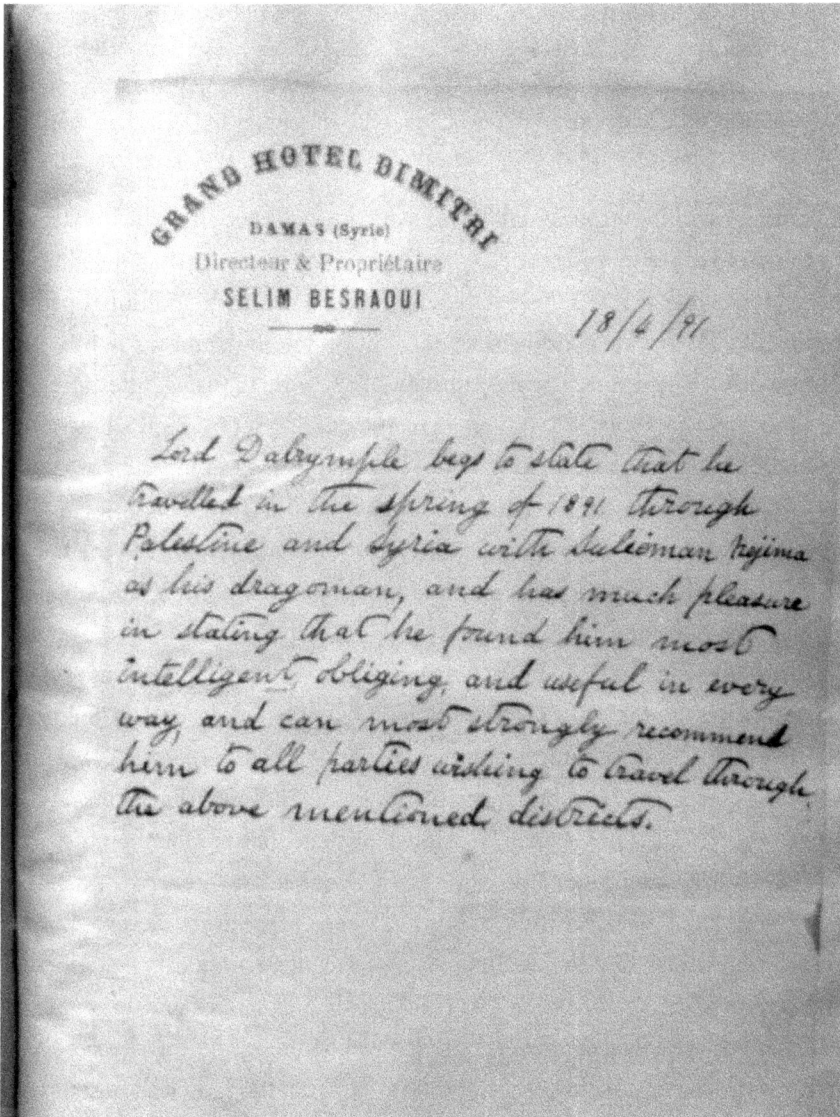

Figure 14: Testimonial letter from Lord Dalrymple. © Rachel Mairs.

Rev Williams' letter is also signed by E. H. Pierce of Rehoboth, Massachusetts. Another member of the party, as can be seen from the letter he wrote at Beirut on the same day, was John M. Barnett of Washington, Pennsylvania, accompanied by his daughter, Marguerite. The Barnetts give some idea of the full itinerary on which Solomon Negima had accompanied the group:

> I cheerfully commend Mr Solomon Negima as a prudent, efficient, intel-
> ligent and gentlemanly Dragoman to all who may desire his services. With my
> daughter and others in one of H. Gaze's and Son's parties, I made the trip from
> Jerusalem to Jericho and from Jerusalem to Beirut by way of Baalbek in April
> 1891. (Negima 1885–1933: SN56, 29 April 1891)

Solomon Negima's testimonial book, which I acquired from a bookseller
in the United States, offers a rare opportunity to access a dragoman's own
perspective. It contains sixty-five letters from clients, with additional papers
relating to the private and business dealings of Solomon and his family. The
earliest letters date to 1885, the latest to 1933, with the latest attestation of
Solomon's own activity as a dragoman in 1903. It has not been possible for me
to find out anything of the book's whereabouts from 1933 to its discovery at
an estate sale in or near Rogue River, Oregon, in the late 1990s (information
courtesy of Dan and Patty Baumgartner). To add a further twist to the tale of
the book's wanderings, I purchased it on eBay in 2014. I intend to publish it
fully in due course.

The book is leather bound, in octavo format, with plain pages onto which
Solomon has pasted letters and photographs – including one of Solomon
taken by the noted photographer Sir Benjamin Stone (1838–1914) whose
archive is kept in the Library of Birmingham. Most of the letters are in
English, with a few in German or Arabic. His clients were for the most part
British or American, but some came from Canada, New Zealand, Australia,
Germany and France. A predictably high percentage were clergymen and
missionaries travelling to see Biblical sites, but there were a fair number of
military men, independent ladies, politicians of all stripes and the types of
Midwestern captains of industry satirized by contemporary travel writers ('At
home he is unquestionably IT'; Ade 1906: 3–5). That he showed these letters to
prospective clients may be seen from the fact that at least two examples were
written on the back of previous notes. In a few places, Solomon has written
annotations over the letters and in the margins of the book. His handwriting is
formal, but not particularly confident. He practises writing his own name, and
that of his daughter, Lulu, using clients' letters as a model – or perhaps Lulu
practises her own. Inside the front cover of the book, partially over a letter,
he has written 'Testimonial Book of Dragoman Solomon N. Negima'. On
the facing page, under the heading 'This is the Sertificat Book of Dragoman

Solomon Negima', are two photographs captioned 'A Naite on the Foot of Mount Harmon' and 'Ande of the Trepp in Bairut'. Inside the back cover are two photographs of Solomon himself, taken and sent to him by clients (Figure 15: Photographs of Solomon Negima).

What little we know of Solomon Negima's early life comes from what he told the people he guided, and what they in turn chose to record in their letters and journals. One of the great pleasures of working through Solomon's testimonial book has been tracking down accounts written by his clients, published and unpublished, and identifying him therein, either by name, or as an anonymous dragoman. Rev Joseph Llewellyn Thomas, who travelled with Solomon in 1889, recorded that he was born at Ramoth-Gilead, and that his father was from Nazareth and his mother from Moab (Thomas 1890: 87). Ellen E. Miller, whom he escorted in 1888, thought him 'a many-sided individual': a Syrian Roman Catholic, educated at a German Protestant mission school, who spoke excellent English and even better German, and who had served

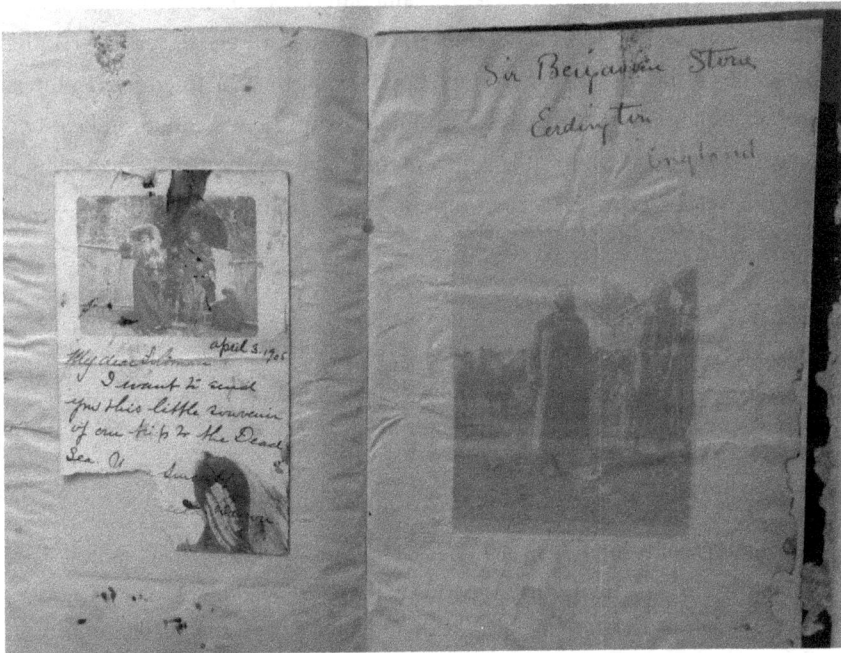

Figure 15: Photographs of Solomon Negima, from inside the back cover of his testimonial book. © Rachel Mairs.

with the British army in the Sudan (Miller 1891: 162). I shall dwell at greater length on Rev Thomas' and Miss Miller's accounts below. Earlier clients, as a rule, found him more inclined to be chatty and share details of his own life than later ones, who commented on his 'quiet, unassuming manner' (Negima 1885–1933: SN13, 1895) and 'calm temperament' (Negima 1885–1933: SN16, 1893).

Interpreter on the Nile

Solomon's documented career begins in 1885, with the British army in Egypt and Sudan. In 1884–5, an expedition was undertaken to relieve General Gordon and his garrison at Khartoum, where they were besieged by the forces of the Mahdi, a messianic leader. The expeditionary force was composed of soldiers and support staff from across the British Empire, including West African and Canadian Mohawk boatmen (Benn 2009), as well as large numbers of Egyptians and Sudanese. One British veteran recorded that his boat at the third cataract held two Canadian *voyageurs*, six West African Kroomen, an Arab guide, a Syrian interpreter and an English servant (Butler 1887: 171). (It may be too fanciful to suppose that the unnamed Syrian interpreter was Solomon.) Along with testimonials from clients, Solomon kept two letters of reference from British officers under whom he had served, which reveal the details of his participation in the campaign:

Shepheard's Hotel, Cairo 15.7.85

Solomon Negimah has served with the 9th Transport Com up the Nile during the last ten months. He was engaged as Headman but has really acted as Interpreter all through – he speaks English well and can read and write Arabic. I have found him an intelligent well informed man and strictly honest – rather a rare quality among interpreters.
H. P. Leach Capt RE. (Negima 1885–1933: SN6; Figure 16)

The bearer Solomon Negimae has been employed as Headman in No. 9 Company C & T Corps during the period of the Nile Expedition and now leaves the Company on its return to Cairo, he can read and write Arabic, and can speak English fairly well, and would make a very fair interpreter. He has worked well and given every satisfaction. –

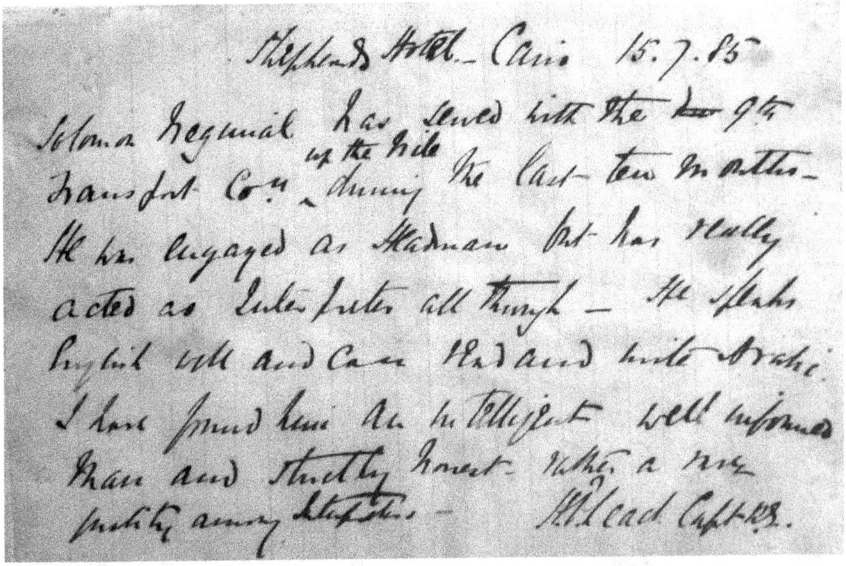

Figure 16: Testimonial letter from Capt Leach. © Rachel Mairs.

Edw. J. J. Teale Capt. & DACG

Comdg 9th Co. C T Corps

Cairo 17. 7. 85 (Negima 1885–1933: SN39; Figure 17)

Solomon was a keen raconteur and later regaled clients with stories of his participation in the campaign:

> We left Jerusalem shortly after noon. By 'we' I mean my dragoman Suleiman, the muleteer Hamed, and myself. I think I have been exceedingly fortunate in my dragoman. When he is not pointing out to me some place mentioned in Scripture, and telling me all he knows about it – which is usually a good deal – he entertains me with the recital of his experiences in the Nile Expedition, which are even more stirring than those of Major Mackie. He served in connection with the transport department in the Soudan, and was present at Abu Klea and Metemmeh. He showed me his medals, not that I doubted his word, as dragomans are a very truthful body of men; and I also know from other sources that Suleiman was really present at those battles, and that he was an eye-witness of the death of Colonel Burnaby. So I consider myself fortunate in having secured the services of such an interesting dragoman. ... Before I have done with Suleiman I shall probably know all his history, as he is very communicative, and delights in airing his English, which is remarkably good. (Thomas 1890: 87)

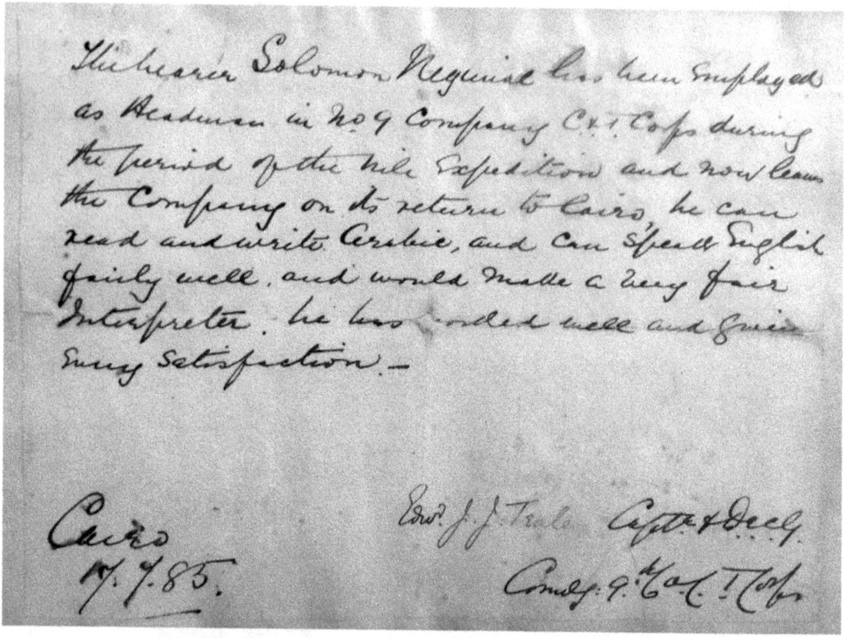

Figure 17: Testimonial letter from Capt Teale. © Rachel Mairs.

Other clients, too, heard tales of the Nile Expedition from Solomon. Miss Miller described his pride at being mistaken for a soldier, and his military-style costume (Miller 1891: 162). An English party in 1895 repeated in their testimonial his claim that he had been 'the only interpreter who accompanied the British army till the campaign was completed', and suggested that his military experience had stood him in good stead in managing a tourist camp and retainers (Negima 1885–1933: SN3). His service with the British army gave Solomon a knack for managing his clients as well as his team, and an understanding of what some of them expected in a 'native servant'. In 1889, he escorted William Stone, author of *Shall We Annex Egypt?* (1884) – a work which is every bit as paternalistic and imperialist as its title suggests. The resulting testimonial records that Solomon 'proved most civil and obliging, and at the same time knew, what Mr. Stone has so rarely found in men of his class, that he was under orders' (Negima 1885–1933: SN55). It is tempting to fantasize an alternative narrative behind these letters, in which Solomon directs the action; and on this occasion it is especially difficult to escape the conclusion that he sized up Stone and knew precisely what kind of relationship to cultivate. Solomon was aware that his participation in the famed Nile Expedition – which arrived, in the end, two days too late to save Gordon – gave him an air of respectability and even glamour in the eyes of his clients. He showed his medals to them (Negima 1885–1933: SN13, 1895), and asked one client to procure an additional medal for him in Cairo (the Khedive's Star, to which he was entitled, but may have lost: Negima 1885–1933: SN28, 1894).

Dragoman in Palestine

At some point between 1885 and 1888, Solomon returned to Palestine and went into business as a tourist dragoman, a natural progression from his role as interpreter on the Nile. The profession of dragoman had changed in the years immediately preceding the start of Solomon's career: an experienced, professional local dragoman in the late 1880s was far more likely to receive clients from a tour company than be in a position to solicit them independently. In 1874, a concerned British traveller in Egypt and Palestine wrote to *The Times* from Beirut on behalf of a group of dragomans, who had recently held a meeting to discuss the current state of their profession, and formed a co-operative (*The Times* 1874: 6). The letter which he enclosed detailed the dragomans' objections to the new monopoly of foreign agencies, and the advantages which they considered independent, local contractors to have over these. In particular, they viewed the advertisements placed by Thomas Cook's in the press as misleading, in their insinuation that only their company could make arrangements for transport such as Nile steamers. The dragomans point out that their rates undercut Cook's by a considerable margin; that they offer travellers independence to choose their own itinerary; that professional, experienced local dragomans bring invaluable local knowledge. The letter is signed by seventeen dragomans, from Beirut, Jerusalem, Jaffa and Alexandria. Cook's naturally responded in the letter pages of *The Times*, protesting that their dominance of the market was due to excellent services and fair competition, while acknowledging the reality of their near monopoly.

Tourists appear almost always to have engaged Solomon's services through the intermediary of one of the large, foreign-owned tour agents, such as Thomas Cook's, Henry Gaze's, or the operation of Rolla Floyd. From at least

1889, Solomon worked most closely with Floyd, an American dragoman based in Jaffa, although some clients also came to him from Thomas Cook's. The relationship with Floyd led to further opportunities for Solomon and his family in later years.

Floyd had settled in the Holy Land with followers of the Reverend George J. Adams, who established a colony at Jaffa in 1866 to prepare for the Second Coming (Holmes 2003 is an idealistic whitewash of the affair). Adams was a controversial figure: sometime Mormon elder, actor and tireless self-publicist. Despite press reports which claimed that he was a charlatan, he attracted a group of acolytes from New England who sold their property and moved to Palestine with him. The colony was a disaster. Mark Twain, who encountered some of its members as they fled Jaffa in 1867, called it a 'complete fiasco' (Twain 1869: 613). Adams was revealed as a fraud and a drunk, and the land was unproductive. Colonists left in droves.

Among the few who remained was Rolla Floyd, a carpenter who seems to have migrated to Palestine more for economic opportunities than out of any religious conviction. His letters home to family in the United States, collected by Helen Palmer Parsons, reveal a man who worked hard and adapted to local circumstances in order to build a life in Palestine (Parsons 1981). In 1869, he secured a contract with the Turkish government to manage stage coaches between Jaffa and Jerusalem. He learnt to speak Arabic fluently and read up on the history of Palestine in order to set himself up in business as a tourist dragoman. Floyd apprenticed in the trade by working as the assistant of a local dragoman named El Hani, in whose company the American social campaigner Frances E. Willard encountered him in 1870 (Gifford 1995: 343; this same Hani may also have been one of the signatories of the 1874 letter to *The Times*), but was able to benefit from the prejudice of travellers that local guides were less trustworthy than fellow Americans or Europeans (letter of 18 July, 1870, Parsons 1981: 12–13). His business was a great success. He worked for Thomas Cook and Son from 1876 until a falling out in 1881, and, having established himself as an independent contractor, spent the following years poaching as much of their business as he could (Brendon 1991: 139–40).

Floyd mentions in his letters training other dragomans to work for him in conducting travellers through Palestine (11 July 1879, Parsons 1981: 44–5). In a letter of 6 September 1882, commenting on the rising tensions in Egypt, Floyd writes, 'If I was a single man would go [sic] to Egypt and be a Dragoman for some English general' – precisely what Solomon Negima was doing at that time or a little later. We do not know if Floyd and Solomon already knew one another at this point: the first mention of their association is in a letter of 1889 (Negima 1885–1933: SN32). Nor does Floyd ever mention Solomon by name in his letters. We do know that Floyd found it 'very hard to get men who I can trust to act as Dragomen, or take charge of large parties while travelling through the country', and that he valued those he did (letter of 15 November 1888, Parsons 1981: 124).

The testimonial letters show the kind of qualities clients, and employers such as Floyd, prized in Solomon Negima. Often, travellers appear to have started from a perspective very close to that of that of the accounts discussed in Chapter 2: dragomans were rapacious, deceitful, at best a necessary evil of travel in the East. They may have gained these impressions from their own experiences, in Palestine or Egypt, or from the Orientalist clichés of guidebooks and travel journals. To jaded, prejudiced tourists such as these, Solomon seems to have come as a pleasant surprise. The body of letters included in the testimonial book, for showing to prospective clients, was of course self-selecting. Solomon, who could read English, would not have included negative reviews – and, indeed, clients will have known that there was little point in them writing them. George Ade's skit about Mahmoud's testimonial letters (see Chapter 2) is little more than a fantasy of what a frustrated tourist wished he could warn his dragoman's next 'victims'. While we lack negative reviews of Solomon's services – and it is moreover difficult to distinguish tone of voice in some of the letters between Victorian under-statement and 'damning with faint praise' – in many cases there is an implied or explicit contrast with those of other dragomans.

The positive terms which recur most frequently in Solomon's testimonials are 'obliging', 'attentive', 'scrupulously honest', 'painstaking' and 'trustworthy'. Solomon is commended as possessing tact, an even temper and a good sense of humour. Some letters are brief and to the point; others are glowing. Rear Admiral Kirkland of the US Navy thought him 'a success from beginning to end ... I have not met his equal' (Negima 1885–1933: SN7, 1895). His knowledge of English and German is almost always described as fluent. Above all, it was his expert knowledge of the antiquities and ancient sites of the Holy Land, and his ability to relate these to precise passages in the Bible, which won him admiration and appreciation. As a local Christian, educated in a European Christian school, foreign Christian clients may well have been more likely to trust him and treat him with greater respect – certainly, his faith gave his opinions on Biblical matters greater authority. A party in 1895 were pleased to find that 'he has an accurate knowledge of the country and its history – but does not plague one with unnecessary information' (Negima 1885–1933: SN3, 1895). A New Zealand family of German extraction had a similar experience, repeated in a double testimonial in English and German: 'He seems a respectable & intelligent man who knows the country well & points out all the places of interest without boring you with too much talk' (Negima 1885–1933: SN10, 1894). Solomon's ability to differentiate between the historical tradition, as understood locally, and the textual (usually Biblical) history given precedence by his clients, also won him positive testimonials, as did his concern with the day-to-day comforts of tourists:

> The entire outfit – horses, tents, food and furniture were better than we expected and the attention and kindness of the camp servants left nothing to be desired. We consider that <u>Sulieman Negima</u>, our Dragoman, is without a superior and if we ever come to Palestine again we shall stipulate that he is to go with us. We have found him well versed in Bible history and careful in his discrimination between history and tradition. (Negima 1885–1933: SN23, 1892)
>
> It is seldom that we give a recommendation as heartily as we give this one of Soliman Negima, Dragoman.
>
> He understands his business thoroughly. He is versed in all the history and traditions of Syria and Palestine and the most careful students of the Bible will value his opinions most highly.
>
> He can be <u>perfectly</u> trusted to make bargains for his party and will give them every advantage of reduced price. We have formed a very high opinion of his character and shall recommend him to our friends as the most desirable Dragoman we have met. (Negima 1885–1933: SN18, 1892)
>
> Solomon has an excellent knowledge of the various places of interest en route and takes great pains to point them out to travellers: his explanations are not of the usual showman's type but are marked by thought and reason. ... He has the advantage very unusual in this country of a calm temperament and I have the greatest pleasure in recommending him as a thoroughly competent and satisfactory dragoman, with whom it is a pleasure to travel. (Negima 1885–1933: SN16, 1893)

Although very much products of their time, none of the letters are so crude as to cast Solomon Negima as a servile, inflexible, irrational Oriental – which is not what their writers wanted from a dragoman in any case. But there is also a tension here between the submission expected of an Arab (albeit Christian) servant to a Euro-American employer of high social status, and the stereotypically non-Oriental behaviour and qualities valued by clients and demonstrably present in Solomon: such as tact, conciseness in speech, efficiency and critical judgement. Solomon's deference to his clients' wishes and preferred way of doing things made a positive impression, but many also appreciated a guide who could be an intelligent companion. As with the case of William Stone (Negima 1885–1933: SN55), who preferred 'men of his class' to know that they were 'under orders', we must suppose that Solomon was able to gauge each individual client's preference and adjust his manner accordingly.

Letters from some clients indicate a deeper relationship than simply that between guide and tourist, even – to the extent to which it was possible between people of such different social classes and walks of life – friendship. Some clients stayed in touch over the years, enquiring after Solomon's family and sending news of old travelling companions (for example, J. S. Thompson of Lacon, Illinois: Negima 1885–1933: SN30, 1889; SN44, 1893; SN4, 1894). The American labour leader and social campaigner, Alexander Troup, wrote a friendly letter from Cairo, enclosing with it his more formal testimonial (Negima 1885–1933: SN28, 1894). To the modern reader, one of the most interesting of Solomon's clients is Rev Charles T. Walker (1858–1921) of Augusta, Georgia, a renowned African American preacher, who had been born into slavery (Floyd 1902). Rev Walker was the author of *A Colored Man Abroad* (Walker 1892), in which he recorded his observations both of life in Europe and the East and of his own reception there. He was an observer of the East who was himself also very conscious of being observed and stereotyped (see Klatzker 1987 on other nineteenth-century African American travellers in the region). Rev Walker wrote to Solomon after he had returned to the United States, asking for his help in sending some souvenirs of the Holy Land, and reminding him of how they had swapped hats with one another (Negima 1885–1933: SN43, 1892). Solomon's 'red cap' is probably the tarboosh which Rev Walker wears in a photograph taken shortly after his return from his travels (Floyd 1902: 146; Figure 18). D. Ford Goddard, author of testimonial

REV. CHARLES T. WALKER, ON HIS RETURN FROM HIS TRIP TO THE
HOLY LAND, AGE THIRTY THREE YEARS.

Figure 18: Rev Charles T. Walker, wearing Solomon Negima's red tarboosh. Floyd 1902, 146.

SN16, from which I quoted above, also wrote to Solomon after his return home (Figure 19). He had promised to help him in his continuing professional development as an informed and erudite dragoman by sending him a book about the antiquities of Palestine:

> I remember you quite well and often think of the splendid time we had together last year.
>
> I remember also that I promised a book about coins and antiques, but I have not been able to find such a book – there are many books about coins but not what you want. However I do not despair of finding one yet. (Negima 1885–1933: SN46, 1894)

Solomon evidently took his job seriously. Goddard concludes: 'I hope I shall see you and have a hubble-bubble together. How I should like to ride again through the country, it was splendid'. We do not know if he returned to Palestine, or if he and Solomon met – and smoked nargileh together – again.

Oxford to Palestine and Alone Through Syria

Two tourists who travelled with Solomon Negima left accounts of their journeys in which he features as a prominent secondary character. These were

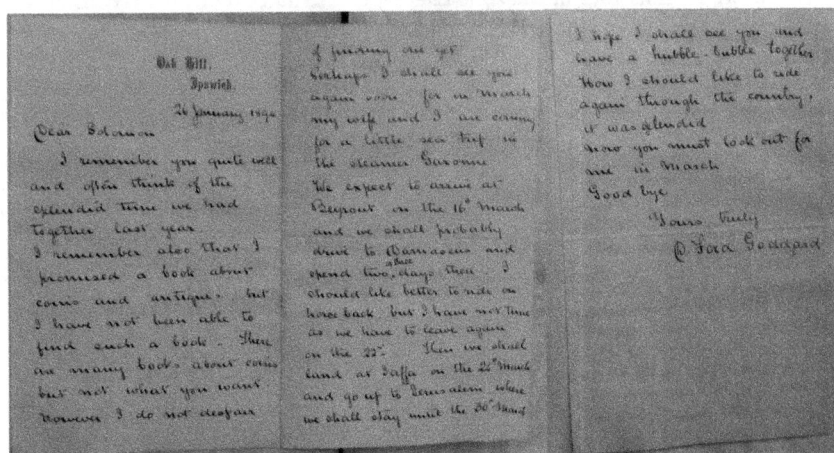

Figure 19: Letter from D. Ford Goddard to Solomon Negima. © Rachel Mairs.

Rev Joseph Llewellyn Thomas (1853–1940), a Welsh Anglican minister and author of *Oxford to Palestine* (1890), and Miss Ellen E. Miller, who published *Alone Through Syria* (1891). They were among Solomon's first clients, in 1888–9. His experiences with them will undoubtedly have influenced his future interactions with – and expectations of – the tourists in his charge.

The title of Miss Miller's account of her travels – *Alone Through Syria* – requires some qualification (on this work, see Kuehn 2014: 99–106). She was alone in the sense that she was without European company, and directed her own itinerary. A contemporary review of the book in the *Guardian* commends 'her wish to move independently, without the distraction or constraint of a large party of companions. To do this she engaged an attendant at Jaffa, by name Solomon, who could talk English freely, and who proved a useful and well-conducted attendant all through her somewhat adventurous journey' (*Guardian*, 1891: 23). Miss Miller's tone is blithely confident, in contrast to her depiction of Solomon as an over-cautious kill-joy. In fact, it is hard not to sympathize with Solomon. This long journey, in the spring of 1888, is the first of which we have record of him acting as dragoman. And Miss Miller was a client who presented Solomon with certain challenges. She owed him a longer and more effusive letter; although the one she wrote, with its business-like tone and gender-neutral signature, is indicative of her straightforward and independent manner:

> On my arrival at Jaffa I engaged Solomon Negim as my personal attendant & after a two months' tour in Palestine I have pleasure in testifying to his constant honesty, straightforwardness & general good conduct.
>
> (Signed by) E. E. Miller
> Batheaston England
> At Beirut 21st May 1888 (Negima 1885–1933: SN48)

As a travel writer, Miss Miller shows a keen interest in people as well as landscapes and antiquities. Her attitude towards the people with whom she came into contact is reasonably nuanced for the period – even if she sometimes calls them 'Easterns' (Miller 1891: 32). She comments on the impressive multilingual talents of her guides, reserving a self-deprecating word of scorn for the British, who are poor enough at learning European languages, 'let alone Arabic' (Miller 1891: 32). She talked with Solomon Negima about topics such as religion, and observed something of his social life. She is also responsible for transmitting to posterity the fact that he snored (Miller 1891: 296). The renowned Assyriologist Rev A. H. Sayce wrote an introduction to her book, in which he praises her engagement with local people and ways of life – in a classically Orientalist manner:

> No book on the East can be successful unless the author possess sympathy with the land and its people. It is necessary to divest ourselves to a certain extent of our Western training, to look at the world from the points of view of the Oriental, if we really wish to understand him, and present a lifelike picture of his habits and thoughts. Miss Miller has shown that she possess this sympathy, and what she has written had accordingly a freshness about which makes it well worth reading, even by those to whom Eastern life is as familiar as that of the West. (Sayce in Miller 1891: vii-viii)

Miss Miller's writings also reveal, however, that, whatever her 'sympathy' for the East, she was not gifted with empathy for her long-suffering dragoman, Solomon Negima.

She engaged Solomon at Jaffa upon the recommendation of Alexander Howard (né Iskander Awwad: Gibson et al. 2013: 58–63), a Maltese-Lebanese hotel keeper and 'General Travelling Contractor', on whose headed notepaper many of Solomon's testimonial letters are written. Miss Miller told Howard her requirements in a guide, and Solomon seems to have fulfilled them well:

> ... a trustworthy man of well-known probity and good behaviour, whom, though I should need him as my guide, I should prefer to look upon as a servant receiving his weekly wage, rather than precisely as a dragoman. Fortunately he had a young man close at hand, who seemed likely to possess the needful qualities, and who owned the promising name of Solomon. I engaged him on Mr. Howard's recommendation, and always found him respectful, well conducted, and strictly honest, though as a guide he was not always quite efficient, because at that time he knew but little about the north country. (Miller 1891: 145)

The only downside was Solomon's apparent timidity, which she remarks upon in several places, and here we can read between the lines of her account. Solomon was still finding his feet as a dragoman, and he was entrusted with a strong-minded client – who also happened to be a lone European female. It is likely that Miss Miller, who was a capable and self-sufficient woman, found his assumptions about her limitations and vulnerability trying. She acknowledged that his concern was for her safety ('I cannot say that Solomon impressed me with *his* valour; indeed, his advice to me was always of a most timid character, and one which I had constantly to combat. Doubtless this timidity was prompted by the sense of his responsible position towards me': Miller 1891: 163), but she appears sometimes to have been unaware of just how vulnerable she was.

Solomon probably found the business of chaperoning a lone Englishwoman in Palestine a baptism of fire; at the very least, Miss Miller was a handful. He had to act as interpreter with a confused and put-upon local maidservant: 'On one or two occasions he emphasized his words by giving the poor girl a good shaking' (Miller 1891: 162). Worse, Miss Miller was constantly getting herself into all sorts of trouble: 'rejoicing' at falling in with a rowdy wedding party in Jericho, where she became the centre of attention, and from which Solomon had to extract her (Miller 1891: 194); catching a cold and telling Solomon that he was responsible for nursing her back to health, otherwise she would return to Europe and his contract would be at an end (Miller 1891: 209); trying to spend some leisure time alone on the Mount of Olives, where Solomon was concerned that 'ill-conditioned Arabs' from the 'neighbouring hovels' would 'molest my solitude' ('Solomon was certainly a nervous man': Miller 1891: 181). On the banks of the Jordan:

> I was thankful to alight, and sought out a cool secluded spot on the river-bank, where I requested to be left undisturbed for an hour at least. Poor Solomon was again very uneasy; I fear he thought that I was contemplating suicide! I had previously spoken about bathing in the Jordan, and here its banks looked certainly very steep and dangerous! (Miller 1891: 206)

To Solomon's probable relief, Miss Miller did not scramble down the bank to bathe in the river. Because she was as fascinated with modern Palestine as she was with the ancient Holy Land, she took every opportunity to engage with local people – particularly if they were in some stereotypically Oriental, picturesque setting or engaged in some picturesque activity. She peered into tents: 'How I longed to enter! But Solomon forbade; – I should probably have got there more than I wished for!' (Miller 1891: 268). She innocently encouraged a hanger-on, another dragoman with whom she was having an interesting conversation, even though Solomon was 'sulky' because 'this man was trying to insinuate himself into my favour in the hope that I might take him on instead of my present attendant' (Miller 1891: 225–6). Miss Miller had no intention of replacing Solomon, but her behaviour was insensitive, and had suggested otherwise.

Solomon was not, as it happened, unadventurous. He wangled admission for his charge to a Roman Catholic monastery under false pretences. Protestants had recently been barred from staying there, but Solomon, a Catholic himself, talked their way in (Miller 1891: 270–1). He remained unimpressed with Miss Miller's Protestant convictions, and she did not succeed in persuading him otherwise, but his ability to debate with her as a fellow Christian created a positive impression. Although confident in his abilities and judgement, he was not above recognising his limitations as a dragoman, and hired another guide for regions with which he was less familiar. He continued to develop in his profession over the years, but this early tour with Miss Miller shows a dragoman who was already adept at managing a client and an itinerary, and who took his responsibilities very seriously. Concern about the repercussions for him if a lone Englishwoman were to come to some harm under his care can never have been far from his mind.

The dance of challenges and compromises between Solomon N. Negima and Ellen E. Miller can be amusing to the reader, but was evidently irritating to both at the time. Both are figures with whom a modern critic, the product of a feminist, postcolonialist tradition, instinctively wants to sympathize: the objectified subaltern and the woman who contravenes expected gender norms. In recent scholarship on European travel in the Orient, such figures – marginalized, objectified and subordinated in their own historical and geographical contexts – have gained a new prominence. Innovative, critical discussions of women travellers – and the intersections between gender, sexuality and imperialism – abound (see, for example, Ghose 1998; Blunt 1994; Bird 2012). Other studies have made use of archival materials to explore the relationships between foreign writers and scholars, and the histori-cally mute local participants in their works and journeys (e.g. Quirke 2010, discussed in Chapter 3). The case of Solomon Negima provides a fascinating opportunity to look at the interaction between two individuals who were each objectified by the dominant contemporary male, European gaze: the woman and the Oriental. Rev Charles T. Walker, the African-American minister, adds another distinctive, ambiguous voice to the mix: an educated American traveller of good social standing, but who was also marked as separate from both Europeans and Arabs, through his race and birth as a slave.

In the autumn of 1889, a year and a half after his travels with Miss Miller, Solomon Negima took on a rather more sedate client. Rev Joseph Llewellyn Thomas was an Oxford-educated Anglican minister, who gave a cheerful recommendation:

> I have great pleasure in stating that headman Solomon Negima acted as my dragoman during a tour from Jerusalem to Haifa in November 1889, and that he gave me entire satisfaction. I found him honest and straightforward, and anxious to please. He speaks English remarkably well, and has an intelligent knowledge of places of interest in Palestine. I heartily recommend him to travellers in the Holy Land.
> J. Ll. Thomas M.A.
> Curate (Negima 1885–1933: SN32)

Oxford to Palestine (1890) covers his travels in Europe and the East. Upon his arrival in Alexandria he gained his first experiences of dragomans:

> Hotel touts and dragomans come down upon you like so many vultures, and sometimes the competition is so keen that disagreeable squabbles occur, and you almost think it preferable to be out at sea at the mercy of the angry waves than at the mercy of an excitable Oriental crowd. (Thomas 1890: 27)

Rev Thomas was overwhelmed at the persistence of the dragomans who approached him with written testimonials – like the one which he would later give Solomon. In Cairo, Moursi Ali followed him to his hotel room, but turned out to be 'an admirable guide, and when, on the expiration of our contract, he asked me to be so kind as to write him a testimonial, I not only readily did so, but spoke of him in the highest possible terms, and made no reference to his habit of waylaying visitors at their bedroom doors' (Thomas 1890: 35). If Solomon had behaved in a similar manner, Rev Thomas would not have mentioned it in his letter.

Thomas makes a point of mentioning 'my dragoman, Suleiman N'jima, who accompanied me north, and whom I found an excellent guide' (Thomas 1890: 85). He found him efficient, good at making the best of rough circumstances and an able interpreter of history, language and culture. He was also proud of his own country, which Rev Thomas found an especially appealing aspect of his character:

> When we came in view of the lake, the dragoman and the muleteer seemed as much charmed with the sight as I was. It is, even apart from its sacred associations, a sublime view. It was a beautifully clear day, and the entire lake could be seen at a glance. Suleiman, when we reached the hill above Tiberias, pointed with evident pride to the view as it burst upon us, and seemed to claim no little credit for having guided me to such a beautiful spot; and, familiar as the sight was to him, he still regarded it with something like rapture. (Thomas 1890: 104)

The writings of travellers such as Rev Thomas and Miss Miller give us more information on Solomon Negima and his personality than the testimonial letters alone, but can they bring us any closer to the dragoman's own voice? Can Solomon escape from the (Orientalist) European gaze? In this chapter, I have deliberately kept names as they appear to us in the sources, in order to highlight a notable contrast. Lord Dalrymple refers to himself in the third person, as does Mr Stone; this was the contemporary upper class convention in such letters. In their books and in contemporary reviews of them, Miss Miller and Rev Thomas are always given their titles. Solomon's surname – variously spelt – appears in some of the letters, and in one or two places in the travel books, but he is far more frequently addressed and referred to by his first name alone. As a servant and a native he is never 'Mr Negima'. In both books and letters, Solomon appears to us through the descriptions of others, presented for the consumption of readers of a similar background and social position. What the testimonial book can offer us is an outside perspective *curated* by Solomon: his own choice of positive descriptions of his services, annotated, in places, with a few words of his own composition.

Floyd House

I noted earlier in this chapter that Solomon's association with Rolla Floyd led to further opportunities. In 1902, Floyd, now seventy years old, bought a house in Jerusalem. After the death of his first wife, Floyd married Mary

Jane Clark Leighton, another survivor of the quasi-Mormon Adams colony at Jaffa. In 1910, Mrs Floyd was baptised by missionaries from the Reorganized Church of Jesus Christ of Latter Day Saints (RLDS), newly arrived from the United States. Floyd was not himself a religious man: his letters make frequent, dismissive reference to 'crazy people' who settled in Jerusalem, and their oddball religious convictions. After his death, in 1911, the RLDS missionaries rented Floyd House from his widow. Solomon, his son Aziz and daughter Olinda, were baptised in the river Jordan by Patriarch Frederick G. Pitt on 25 January 1911. Pitt described them as 'pure Arabs, and good, refined people' (Braby 2008, 49–51). A photograph taken in 1912 shows Solomon, probably in his fifties by this point, and his two adult children, along with other members of the mission (Figure 20: Solomon Negima and his family at Floyd House). The Negima family resided at Floyd House as caretakers, working with a series of RLDS missionaries: Ulysses W. Greene, H. Arthur and Edna Koehler, and Hannah and Rees Jenkins. The Jenkinses stayed in Jerusalem during the First World War, and relations with the Negimas broke down over the question of who had been left in charge of the house.

Figure 20: Solomon Negima (front row, left) with his family and RLDS missionaries, at Floyd House, Jerusalem, 1912 (Braby 2008: 54).

The final mention of Solomon Negima is in a letter of March 1918 (Negima 1885–1933: SN71).

The testimonial book of Solomon N. Negima came into my possession in July 2014. Piecing together the separate, but intertangled, histories of Solomon's clients, family and colleagues will take painstaking work, over months, or more probably years. One question, however, has occupied me above all others, and to this I would already hazard an answer. How did the book come to be in Medford, Oregon?

The clearest voice in the later correspondence attached to the book is that of Olinda, Solomon's daughter – 'Lulu' to her friends. Olinda kept in touch with Edna Koehler and Ulysses W. Greene during the war, and their letters to her make it evident that her dearest wish, expressed in her own letters, was to go to America. The replies from the Americans strike the reader as evasive. Just before embarking at Jaffa on 11 November 1914, Edna Koehler wrote to her, 'If it is Lord's will, Olinda, that you should go to America, I think you will be able to go. But don't forget that there is a work in Palestine to do also, and he may possibly want you to help in that work in your own land, so don't get discouraged' (Negima 1885–1933: SN66). A year later, Ulysses W. Greene, writing from his home at Winter Hill, Massachusetts, enclosed a letter to Olinda with one to her father. He describes America in appealing terms: a green land of pleasant scenery and comfortable living, concluding 'I had hoped that you could have found employment and a good home over here, but the cruel war has upset all plans' (Negima 1885–1933: SN69, 1915).

Did Olinda ever go to America? After some English letters in 1918, the only remaining papers in the little archive are some letters and telegrams in Arabic, dated 1933, addressed to her brother Aziz, relating to business matters. These were in a package accompanying the book. The papers, then, stayed together in Jerusalem until at least that date. Perhaps Olinda or Aziz, or their descendants, did emigrate to America, their identities lost in the records by corrupted spellings or new names. Or perhaps the papers were simply picked up in a junk shop in Jerusalem by a more recent traveller.

7

Conclusion

Edward Robinson (1794–1863), an American biblical scholar, avid explorer and topographer of the Near East and of Palestine in particular, found two major faults with the descriptions of these lands by earlier travellers:

> In the first place, travellers simply followed the footsteps of the monks. It made little difference if they were Catholics or Protestants. Almost all, e.g., in Jerusalem, were entertained in the monasteries. The monks served as their guides; and from that great storehouse of the monasteries they obtained their information. The majority of them were also rather credulous as regards the things that were told them. Thus it comes that their accounts are substantially alike. ... The other mistake was that travellers were ignorant of the Arabic language and could hold intercourse with the people only through interpreters; accordingly they never stepped off from the well-beaten paths, which all their predecessors had trodden. In this way, the valuable traditions, which still continued to live among the people, escaped them. (Benzinger 1903: 585–6)

This book is first and foremost about attitudes towards communication. We have tried to elucidate and address the complex linguistic and cultural concerns of navigating the multi-lingual and multi-cultural society that was the Ottoman Empire in the late nineteenth and early twentieth centuries. Travellers and explorers of the earlier periods, who paved the way for the tourists and archaeologists discussed in this book, understood well that, in order to endure and successfully find one's way in the Orient, one needed not only a command of local language(s) but also knowledge and grasp of cultural traditions. 'Acquaintance of the manners of Arabs' (Hilprecht 1903: 163) was considered essential for effective work and survival in the area. By the late nineteenth century, however, travellers arrived in lands which had long been subject to the European Orientalist gaze, and European imperial domination. Tourists who so wished could experience the modern Orient through their Baedeker, their Cook's itineraries and, of course, their dragoman. The Orient was to be described and depicted to European viewers.

Useful recommendations to tourists travelling to Egypt are to be found in the last section of Chapter VIII ('Advice to Travellers') of Giovanni D'Athanasi's autobiography: knowledge of languages and customs – either by the traveller himself or through a hired interpreter is the ultimate source of successful journey:

> The only means by which this journey can be attempted with any chance of safety and pleasure, is first to accustom the body to bear with ease the extremes of heat and cold, and then to acquire a knowledge of the language and customs of the Arabs. With these two qualifications the traveller will be almost sure of succeeding in his enterprise; without them, he runs the risk of being stopped in the middle of his journey, and obliged to return knowing as little as when he set out. (D'Athanasi 1836a: 114)

> For myself I can say that I never experienced the slightest obstacle in any of my journeys. In short, I repeat, that a man who is not acquainted with the manners and the language of the Arabs, or who in default of that, is not accompanied by an interpreter who knows his business as he ought, will never be able, what ever he may do, to travel with advantage, I do not say to Timbuctoo only, but even in Egypt. (D'Athanasi 1836a: 114–15)

Although blending in – at least superficially from the purely visual point of view, i.e. to dress according to the local customs – was long believed to be an important part of a successful journey in the Orient, a resourceful D'Athanasi gives unexpected advice to the European travellers in the East:

> Whilst on this subject I would also observe, that it will be of advantage to the traveller to appear in a European dress; for as the Turks are in the habit of committing acts of violence on the Arabs, the latter whenever they see any one approaching in Oriental costume take to flight as they would from death. On the other hand, whenever they see the European dress, men, women, children, and even the aged are instantly on the alert; some offer you antiquities for sale, others bring you bread, milk, butter, &c. and there are some who make a business of letting out donkeys for hire. In fact, with the European dress a

man will be sure to obtain ready access every where, to see everything that is to be seen, and to be well treated by every one he may meet; whilst on the contrary, habited in Oriental garb he will run the risk of being starved to death (D'Athanasi 1836a: 115).

For many archaeologists, on the other hand, learning Arabic or Turkish to a high standard and understanding and appreciating the local customs was essential for conducting fieldwork and dealing with the Ottoman authorities. It is worth taking a little time to look at some earlier examples of European antiquarians in the East who learned languages for themselves, and for whom 'passing as a local' was part of the adventure.

Claudius James Rich (1787–1821), a British businessman, traveller and explorer of Babylonian and Assyrian ruins, seems to have had a particular gift for languages, and having spent 'more than three years in the different parts of Levant,' acquired almost perfect Italian, Turkish and Arabic:

> His knowledge of the Turkish language and manners was so thorough that while in Damascus not only did he enter the grand mosque 'in the disguise of a Mameluke,' but his host, an honest Turk, who was captivated with his address, eagerly entreated him to settle at that place, offering him his interest and his daughter in marriage. (Hilprecht 1903: 26)

Likewise, James Silk Buckingham (1786–1855), a Cornish writer, journalist and traveller, found it safer and more convenient to adhere to 'native ways,' adopting 'the dress, manners, and language of the country for the sake of greater safety and convenience' (Hilprecht 1903: 36). In order to live, but, more importantly, to be able to productively work in the Orient, one had to be adequately prepared. A French naturalist and explorer, Paul-Émile Botta (1802–70), was sent as a consul to Mosul in 1842. A preceding long residency in Egypt, Yemen and Syria:

> undertaken regardless of difficulties or the dangers of climate, solely to further his scientific pursuits, had eminently adapted him for an appointment in the East. He could assimilate himself to the habits of the people; was conversant with their language; possessed energy of character; and was besides an intelligent and practiced observer. (Hilprecht 1903: 73)

In order to prepare himself for his journey, Austen Henry Layard (1817–94), diplomat, traveller, archaeologist and explorer:

had mastered the Arabic letters, picked up a little of the Persian language, taken lessons in the use of sextant from a retired captain of the merchant service, and even hastily acquired a superficial medical knowledge of the treatment of wounds and certain Oriental diseases. (Hilprecht 1903: 89)

... he was well acquainted with the life and manners of the Arabs, and not unfamiliar with the peculiarities of 'Iraq el-'Arabi as a whole. For in connection with his early adventures in Luristan and Khuzistan he had visited Baghdad repeatedly, and in Arab or Persian disguise he had travelled even among the lawless tribes of the districts adjoining the two rivers to the east and west as far down as Qorna and Basra. (Hilprecht 1903: 157)

Hormuzd Rassam (1826–1910), a native Assyrian, Christian and an Ottoman subject, trained by Layard himself, was – from the Western colonial point of view – an ideal archaeologist and explorer:

In the school of Layard excellently trained and prepared for his task, as a native of Mosul entirely familiar with the language and character of the Arabs, through his previous connections deeply interested in the undertaking, and after a long contact with Western civilization thoroughly impregnated with the English spirit of energy, he was an ideal explorer ... needed to carry the work in the Assyrian ruins to a successful conclusion. (Hilprecht 1903: 129)

Figures such as Petrie and Woolley should be viewed in the context of this long history of engagement with Eastern (and Western) languages and cultures by serious students of history and archaeology. Some archaeologists, on the other hand, were as infected with romanticized notions of the Orient as any tourist. T. E. Lawrence, in his Arab robes, explaining his fair colouring as due to Circassian heritage, was the heir of adventurers and anthropologists such as Richard Burton (1821–90) or Edward Lane (1801–76) as much as of any antiquarian. But he was also the product of Western-based structures for instruction in Arabic. Rev Naser Odeh taught him in Oxford, and Fareedah el-Akle at an American mission, long before Dahoum in the desert.

In this book we have explored several case studies of Anglophone tourists and archaeologists who spent time in Egypt, the Levant and Mesopotamia and who made explicit and detailed (or fleeting and surprisingly dry) references in their published (and unpublished) writings and field notes to the challenges of communication with Arabic and Turkish speakers. Some eventually learnt to speak Arabic competently, others did not, but all were, at some point, dependent on the services of intermediaries – dragomans and guides. Through the centuries, interpreters have been considered liminal figures living between two (or more) worlds. Individuals capable of speaking more than one language and who turned this ability into a professional or semi-professional occupation seemed to incite a curious psychological reaction from others. Because of their ability to speak several languages they defied basic categorization and did not seem to belong to one particular cultural group, and therefore could not be completely trusted; moreover, they were thought to be prone to treachery (Karttunen 1994; Mairs 2011, with relevant bibliography). In recent times, local interpreters for foreign military forces in Afghanistan and Iraq have been subject to violent reprisals from among their own communities, for their 'treachery' to their language and culture. Language and language mediation in conflicts from Yugoslavia to Korea to Northern Ireland have received scholarly attention (Footitt and Kelly, 2012).

In addition to an overview of a variety of multi-lingual individuals who at one time or another served as dragomans, we have provided two portraits of such individuals. A 19-year-old, Daniel Z. Noorian, an Armenian from Sert, hired as an interpreter by the Wolfe Expedition, by picking up additional chores and by becoming indispensable, managed to turn out to be much more than that – a trusted teammate and assistant. Issues of trust also underlie the creation of Solomon N. Negima's scrapbook: by collecting letters from the esteemed clients he created a 'portfolio,' tangible proof that he could be trusted.

Eventually, our two interpreters, Negima and Noorian, followed very different careers. The former remained an interpreter and built a successful business in the 'Land of the Bible', catering to tourists, many of whom were people of wealth and status. An old association with an American dragoman, Rolla Floyd, led to further opportunities for Solomon and his family, as caretakers for a mission in Jerusalem. When war broke out, however, the Americans left, and the Negimas were forced to stay. Noorian took a different path. Having encountered the first American archaeologists trying to get in on the action in the Near East, he understood early on that an ever-growing demand for antiquities in general and for the Near Eastern ones in particular had to be met. Having developed a network of agents and suppliers in the Orient, and later in Europe, he became a successful antiquities dealer in New York and New Jersey.

This book, which derives from our ongoing project on the social roles of interpreters in antiquity, is by no means an exhaustive study of language mediation, and the role of the dragoman, in the late nineteenth and early twentieth centuries. It offers, we hope, some limited insight into the linguistic and cultural gaps between visitors and locals in Egypt and the Near East, and the intermediaries through which these were (sometimes) bridged. Stories such as those of Daniel Z. Noorian and Solomon N. Negima show that the interpreter does not always have to remain invisible. Archival materials, chance finds of books, papers and photographs, and a fresh perspective on old accounts, all bring us closer to letting the dragoman speak for himself.

References

Ade, G. (1906), *In Pastures New*. New York: McClure, Phillips & Co.

Albee, H. R. (1908), 'The craftsmanship of Zado Noorian: rare and delicate work in silver and semi-precious stones done after the old Armenian fashion'. *The Craftsman*, 15 (3), 358–63.

Alexander, H. C. (1906), *Richard Cadbury of Birmingham*. London: Hodder and Stoughton.

Alexander, H. C. (1920), *Charles M. Alexander: A Romance of Song and Soul-Winning*. London: Marshall.

Allen, S. H. (2011), *Classical Spies: American Archaeologists with the OSS in World War II Greece*. Ann Arbor: University of Michigan Press.

Arnold W. R. (1896), *Ancient-Babylonian Temple Records in the Columbia University Library* (Edited with Transcriptions into Neo-Assyrian Characters) (unpublished doctorial dissertation: Columbia University).

Baedeker (1876), *Palestine and Syria. Handbook for Travellers*. Leipsic: Karl Baedeker.

—(1878), *Egypt: Handbook for Travellers. Part First: Lower Egypt*. Leipsic: Karl Baedeker.

—(1892), *Egypt: Handbook for Travellers. Part Second: Upper Egypt, with Nubia*. Leipsic: Karl Baedeker.

Batcheller, George S. (1907), 'Mohammedan marriage, divorce and domestic relation'. *The North American Review*, 185, 766–76.

Bell, G. L. (1927), *The Letters of Gertrude Bell, Selected and Edited by Lady Bell*. New York: Boni and Liveright.

Benn, C. (2009), *Mohawks on the Nile: Natives among the Canadian Voyageurs in Egypt 1884–1885*. Toronto: Natural Heritage Books.

Benziner, J. (1903), 'Research in Palestine', in H. V. Hilprecht, J. Benzinger, G. Steindorff, F. Hommel and P. Jensen, *Explorations in Bible Lands during the 19th Century*. Philadelphia: A. J. Holman and Company, pp. 578–622.

Bergman, H. J. (1982), 'The diplomatic missionary: John Van Ess in Iraq'. *The Muslim World*, 72 (3–4), 180–196.

Bird, D. (2012), *Travelling in Different Skins: Gender Identity in European Women's Oriental Travelogues, 1850-1950*. Oxford: Oxford University Press.

Blunt, A. (1994), *Travel, Gender, and Imperialism: Mary Kingsley and West Africa*. New York: Guilford Press.

Braby, C. F. (2008), 'Hannah S. Jenkins: RLDS missionary wife in Palestine, 1911–20'. *Journal of Mormon History*, 34 (2), 43–72.

Brendon, P. (1991), *Thomas Cook: 150 Years of Popular Tourism*. London: Secker & Warburg.

Brooklyn Daily Eagle (1896), 'Glass Treasures', 5 April 1896, p. 24.

—(1900), 'Ancient Iridescent Phoenician and Greco-Roman Glass', 25 November 1900, p. 3.

Budge, E. A. W. (1897), *Cook's Tourists' Handbook for Egypt, the Nile, and the Desert*. London: T. Cook & Son.

Butler, W. F. (1887), *The Campaign of the Cataracts; being a personal narrative of the great Nile expedition of 1884-5*. London: Sampson Low, Marston, Searle & Rivington.

Carey, M. L. M. (1863), *Four Months in a Dahabëeh: Or, Narrative of a Winter's Cruise on the Nile*. London: L. Booth.

Carswell, J. (1982), 'A la recherche du temps perdu', in Collectif (eds), *Archéologie au Levant. Recueil à la mémoire de R. Saidah*. Lyon: Maison de l'Orient et de la Méditerranée Jean Pouilloux, pp. 481–96.

Christie, A. (2001a) [1936], *Murder in Mesopotamia*, in A. Christie, *Poirot in the Orient*. London: HarperCollins Publishers.

—(2001b) [1937], *Death on the Nile*, in A. Christie, *Poirot in the Orient*. London: HarperCollins Publishers.

—(2001c) [1938], *Appointment with Death*, in A. Christie, *Poirot in the Orient*. London: HarperCollins Publishers.

—(2010) [1977], *An Autobiography*, London: Harper Collins.

Christie Mallowan, A. (1999) [1946], *Come, tell me how you live*. London: HarperCollins Publishers.

Dahlberg, B. T. and O'Connell, K. G. (eds) (1989), *Tell el-Hesi: The Site and the Expedition*. Winona Lake, IN.

Daily Journal (1888). 'To Explore Babylon', 4 August 1888, p. 2.

D'Athanasi, G. (1836a), *A Brief Account of the Researches and Discoveries in Upper Egypt, Made Under the Direction of Henry Salt, Esq. ... To which is Added, a Detailed Catalogue of Mr Salt's Collection of Egyptian Antiquities, Illustrated with Twelve Engravings ... and an Enumeration of those Articles Purchased For the British Museum*. London: John Hearne.

—(1836b), *Exhibition Catalogue of Giovanni d'Athanasi's Collection of Egyptian Antiquities, Arranged by Leigh Sotheby, Exeter Hall, Strand*. London: J. Davy.

—(1836c), *Catalogue of a Collection of Egyptian Antiquities, the Property of Giovanni d'Athanasi ... which will be Sold by Auction by Mr. Sotheby and Son, at their House, Wellington Street, Strand on Saturday, the 5th of March, 1836*. London: J. Davy.

—(1837), *Catalogue of the Very Magnificent and Extraordinary Collection of Egyptian Antiquities, the Property of Giovanni d'Athanasi which will be Sold by Auction by Mr. Leigh Sotheby at his House, 3, Wellington Street, Strand on Manday, March 13th 1837, and Six Following Days (Sunday Excepted)*. London: J. Davy for Leigh Sotheby.

—(1845), *Catalogue of the Residue of a Most Interesting Collection: Egyptian Antiquities which will be Sold by Auction by Messrs S. Leigh Sotheby & Co. ... at their house, 3, Wellington Street, Strand, on Thursday, July 17th, 1845*. London: J. Davy for Leigh Sotheby.

Dirr, A. and Lyall, W. H. (1904), *Dirr's Colloquial Egyptian Arabic Grammar, for the use of Tourists* (Colloquial Egyptian Arabic grammar). London: Henry Frowde.

Drower, M. S. (1995), *Flinders Petrie: A Life in Archaeology* (2nd edn). Madison: University of Wisconsin Press.

Eden, F. (1871), *The Nile without a Dragoman*. London: H. S. King & Co.

Ehrlicher, C. (1912), 'Around-the-world letters'. *The American Journal of Nursing*, 12, 429–31.

El Kholy, N. (2001), 'Romances and Realities of Travellers', in P. Starkey and J. Starkey (eds), *Unfolding the Orient: Travellers in Egypt and the Near East*. Reading: Ithaca, pp. 261–75.

Elias, M. (1935?), *Le dragoman – vocabulaire du voyageur: français, anglais, arabe / The Dragoman – Traveller's Vocabulary: English, French, Arabic*. Cairo: Elias' Modern Press.

Elmenfi, F. (2013), 'Retranslation of *Orientalism*: reading Said in Arabic'. *International Journal of Social, Management, Economics and Business Engineering*, 7 (12), 1834–41.

Fagan, B. (1979), *Return to Babylon. Travelers, Archaeologists, and Monuments in Mesopotamia*. Boston, Toronto: Little, Brown and Company.

Fatah, B. (1912), *Méthode directe pour l'enseignement de l'arabe parlé, rédigée conformément aux nouveaux programmes* (2nd edn). Alger: A. Jourdan.

Finati, G. (1830), *Narrative of the life and adventures of Giovanni Finati, native of Ferrara, who, under the assumed name of Mahomet, made the campaigns against the Wahabees for the recovery of Mecca and Medina; and since acted as interpreter to European travellers in some parts least visited of Asia and Africa*. Translated from the Italian, as dictated by himself, and edited by William John Bankes, Esq. London: John Murray, Albemarle-Street.

Floyd, S. X. (1902), *Life of Charles T. Walker, D. D.*. Nashville: National Baptist Publishing Board.

Footitt, H. and Kelly, M. (eds) (2012), *Languages and the Military: Alliances, Occupation and Peace Building*. Basingstoke; New York: Palgrave Macmillan.

Forbes, D. (1868), *A Grammar of the Arabic Language: Intended more especially for the use of young men preparing for the East India Civil Service, and also for the use of self-instructing students in general*. London: Wm. H. Allen.

Fry, G. T. (1918), 'Egyptian scenes'. *The Art World*, 3, 368–70.

Garnett, D. (ed.) (1938), *The Letters of T. E. Lawrence*. London: Jonathan Cape.

Gayed, R. ([n.d.]), *The Dragoman in the Pocket (My Arabic leader)*. Cairo: Anglo Egyptian Bookshop.

Ghose, I. (1998), *Women Travellers in Colonial India: The Power of the Female Gaze*. Delhi; New York: Oxford University Press.

Gibson, S., Shapira, Y. and Chapman, R. L. (2013), *Tourists, Travellers and Hotels in 19th-century Jerusalem*. Leeds: Maney Publishing.

Gifford, C. D. S. (ed.) (1995), *Writing Out My Heart: Selections from the Journal of Frances E. Willard, 1855-96*. Urbana: University of Illinois Press.

Goodknight, E. L. (1891), 'From the Holy Land'. *Miami Helmet (Piqua, Ohio)*, 2 July, p. 8.

Goodrich-Freer, A. (1904), *Inner Jerusalem*. New York: Dutton.

Green, A. O. (1883), *Practical Arabic Grammar*. Cairo: Boulack Printing Office.

Gregory, D. (1995), 'Between the book and the lamp: imaginative geographies of Egypt, 1849–50'. *Transactions of the Institute of British Geographers*, 20, 29–57.

—(1999), 'Scripting Egypt: Orientalism and the cultures of travel', in J. Duncan and D. Gregory (eds), *Writes of Passage: Reading Travel Writing* London; New York: Routledge, pp. 114–50.

Guardian (1891), 'Review of Miller', 3 June, p. 23.

Hands, C. (1898), 'Tyranny of the Dragoman'. *The Church Weekly*, 25 November, p. 18.

Harfouch, J. (1894), *Le drogman arabe, ou, Guide pratique de l'arabe parlé en caractères figurés: pour le Syrie, la Palestine et l'Egypte*. Beyrouth: Libr. de l'imprimerie catholique.

Hassam, A. (1883), *Arabic Self-Taught, or the Dragoman for Travellers in Egypt*. London: Franz Thimm.

Hassam, A. and Odeh, N. (1915), *Arabic Self-Taught. (Syrian.) With English phonetic pronunciation* (Marlborough's self-taught series). London: E. Marlborough & Co.

Herodotus (trans.Waterfield, R.) (1998), *The Histories*. Oxford: Oxford University Press.

Hilpreht, H.V. (1903), 'The Resurrection of Assyria and Babylonia', in H. V. Hilprecht, J. Benzinge, G. Steindorf, F. Hommel and P. Jensen, *Explorations in Bible Lands during the 19th Century*, Philadelphia: A. J. Holman and Company, pp. 1–578.

Hilprecht, H. V. (ed.) (1908), *The So-Called Hilprecht-Peters Controversy*. Part I: *Proceedings of the Committee Appointed by the Board of Trustees of the University of Pennsylvania to Act as a Court of Inquiry*. Part II: *Supplemental Documents, Evidence and Statement*. Philadelphia: A.J. Holman and Company.

Holmes, R. M. (2003), *Dreamers of Zion, Joseph Smith and George J. Adams: Conviction, Leadership, and Israel's Renewal*. Brighton; Portland, OR: Sussex Academic Press.

Horner, A. S. and Horner, J. B. (1873), *Walks in Florence*, Volume II. London: Strahan & Co.

Jastrow, M. Jr. (1916), 'William Hayes Ward (1835–1916)'. *Journal of the American Oriental Society*, 36, 233–42.

Kalfatovic, M. R. (ed.) (1992), *Nile Notes of a Howadji: A Bibliography of Travelers' Tales from Egypt, from the Earliest Time to 1918*. Metuchen, NJ: Scarecrow Press.

Karttunen, F. (1994), *Between Worlds: Interpreters, Guides, and Survivors*. New Brunswick, NJ: Rutgers University Press.

Keats, J. (1848), *Love, Letters and Literary Remains of John Keats*, R. M. Milnes (ed.), Volume II. London: Edward Moxton, Dover Street.

Kelly, R. T. (1902), *Egypt Painted and Described*. London: Black.

Klatzker, D. (1987), *American Christian Travelers in the Holy Land, 1821–1939*, Unpublished Thesis. Temple University.

Kuehn, J. (2014), *A Female Poetics of Empire: From Eliot to Woolf*. New York: Routledge.

Kuklik, B. (1996), *Puritans in Babylon: The Ancient Near East and American Intellectual Life, 1880–1930*. Princeton: Princeton University Press.

Kuneralp, S. (1997), 'Évolution de la charge de dragoman du Divan imperial Durant le XIXe siècle', in F. Hitzel (ed.), *Istanbul et les langues orientales*. Paris; Montréal: L'Harmattan, pp. 479–83.

Larzul, S. and Messaoudi, A. (eds) (2013), *Manuels d'arabe d'hier et d'aujourd'hui: France et Maghreb, XIXe-XXIe siècle*. Paris: Éditions de la Bibliothèque nationale de France.

Lewis, B. (2004), *From Babel to Dragomans. Interpreting the Middle East*. Oxford: University Press.

M. G. H. (1888), 'Embroidery in America'. *The Art Amateur*, 18, 123.

Mack, J. E. (1976), *A Prince of our Disorder: The Life of T. E. Lawrence*. London: Weidenfeld and Nicolson.

Madox, J. (1834), *Excursions in the Holy Land, Egypt, Nubia, Syria, &c. Including a Visit to the Infrequented District of the Haouran*, 2 vols. London: Richard Bentley.

Mairs, R. (2011), 'Translator, *traditor*: The interpreter as traitor in Classical tradition'. *Greece and Rome*, 58 (1), 64–81.

Mallowan, M. (2001) [1977], *Mallowan's Memoirs: Agatha and the Archaeologist*. London: HarperCollins Publishers.

Mansel, P. (1996), *Constantinople. City of the World's Desire, 1453–1924*. New York: St. Martin's Press.

McLain, L. (1965), 'Mystery of a masterpiece'. *Salt Lake Tribune*, Sunday, 13 June, p. 6.

Meade, C. W. (1974), *Road to Babylon. Development of U. S. Assyriology*. Leiden: Brill.

Mengi, F. (1823), *Histoire de l'Égypte sous le Gouvernement de Mohammed-Aly*, 2 vols. Paris: Chez Arthus Bertrand, Librarie.

Miller, E. E. (1891), *Alone Through Syria*. London: Kegan Paul, Trench, Trübner.

Miṣrī, Khalīfah ibn Maḥmūd al- (1850), *Qalā'id al-jumān fī fawā'id al-tarjumān/ Instructions aux drogmans*. Būlāq: al-Maṭbaʻah al-ʻĀmirah.

Mousa, S. (1966), *T. E. Lawrence: An Arab View*. Oxford: Oxford University Press.

Museum of Fine Arts Boston (2015), *Attic red figure fragment of a rhyton*. Available from: www.mfa.org/collections/object/attic-red-figure-fragment-of-a-rhyton-154043 (accessed 15 September 2014).

Nakhlah, Y. (1874), *New Manual of English and Arabic Conversation*. Boulack: The Khedive's Press.

Negima, S. (1885–1933), *Testimonial Book of Dragoman Solomon N. Negima*. Unpublished, private collection of Rachel Mairs, SN1–82.

New York Times (1903) 'Art Note', 6 May 1903, p. 8.

—(1905) 'Stone Tablet a Manuscript. Appraiser Defines Status of Inscription from Assyrian Tomb', 26 March 1905, p. 14.

—(1922) 'Old Painting Sale Ends', 23 March 1922, p. 12.

Noorian, J. Z. (1909), 'The spirit of Oriental craftsmanship'. *The Craftsman*, 16 (2), 240–2.

Oliver A. (2014), *American Travelers on the Nile: Early U.S. Visitors to Egypt, 1774–1839*. Cairo: The American University in Cairo Press.

Osborne, C. (1982), *The Life and Crimes of Agatha Christie: A Biographical Companion to the Works of Agatha Christie*. New York: St. Martin's Press.

Panzac, D. (1997), 'Les dragomans pour voyageurs dans l'Orient du XIXe siècle', in F. Hitzel (ed.), *Istanbul et les langues orientales*. Paris; Montréal: L'Harmattan, pp. 451–76.

Parker, A. K. (1896), 'Jerusalem and Thereabouts', *The Biblical World*, 7, 342–51.

Parkinson, R. B. (2009), *Reading Ancient Egyptian Poetry: Among Other Histories*. Chichester and Malden, MA: Wiley-Blackwell.

Parsons, H. P. (ed.) (1981), *Letters from Palestine: 1868-1912*. Self-published.

PEFQ (Quarterly Statement of the Palestine Exploration Fund) (1893), London: Palestine Exploration Fund.

—(1895), London: Palestine Exploration Fund.

Peters, J. P. (1897), *Nippur or Explorations and Adventures on the Euphrates. The Narrative of the University of Pennsylvania Expedition to Babylonia in the years 1888-1890*, Volume II: *Second Campaign*. New York and London: G. P. Putnam's Sons.

—(1898), *Nippur or Explorations and Adventures on the Euphrates. The Narrative of the University of Pennsylvania Expedition to Babylonia in the years 1888-1890*, Volume I: *First Campaign*. New York and London: G. P. Putnam's Sons.

Petrie, W. M. F. (1888), *A Season in Egypt: 1887*. London: Field and Tuer.

—(1892), *Ten Years' Digging in Egypt (1881-1891)*. New York: Revell.

—(1904), *Methods and Aims in Archaeology*. London: Macmillan and Co.

Poe, S. A. (1916), *Ten Months on the Wing*. Roswell, NM: Old Santa Fe Press.

Porter, J. L. (1858), *A Handbook for Travellers in Syria and Palestine*. London: J. Murray.

Pratt, M. L. (2008), *Imperial Eyes: Travel Writing and Transculturation* (2nd edn). London: Routledge.

Quirke, S. (2010), *Hidden Hands: Egyptian Workforces in Petrie Excavation Archives 1880-1924*. London: Duckworth.

Richards, J. C. and Rodgers, T. S. (2001), *Approaches and Methods in Language Teaching*. Cambridge; New York: Cambridge University Press.

Robinson, G. L. (1901a), 'Modern Ḳadesh, or 'Ain Ḳadîs'. *The Biblical World*, 17, 327–38.

—(1901b), 'The newly discovered "high place" at Petra in Edom'. *The Biblical World*, 17, 6–16.

Rogers, R. W. (1900), *A History of Babylonia and Assyria*, 2 vols. New York: Eaton and Mains.

Rothman, E. N. (2009), 'Interpreting dragomans: boundaries and crossings in the Early Modern Mediterranean'. *Comparative Studies in Society and History*, 51 (4), 771–800.

Said, E. W. (1978), *Orientalism*. London: Routledge & Kegan Paul.

—(1999), *Out of Place: A Memoir*. London: Granta.

Salamé, A. V. (1819), *A Narrative of the Expedition to Algiers in the Year 1816, under the command of the Right Hon. Admiral Lord Viscount Exmouth*. London: J. Murray.

Shepheard's (1895), *Cairo and Egypt: A Practical Handbook for Visitors to the Land of the Pharaohs*. Munich: A. Bruckmann for Shepheard's Hotel.

Sherman, A. R. (1915), 'Birds by the wayside, in Egypt and Nubia'. *The Wilson Bulletin*, 27, 369–93.

Spar, I. (1988), *Cuneiform texts in the Metropolitan Museum of Art*, Vol. I: *Tablets, Cones, and Bricks of the Third and Second Millennia B.C.* New York: The Metropolitan Museum of Art.

Spoer, H. H. and Haddad, E. N. (1909), *Manual of Palestinean Arabic for Self-Instruction*. Jerusalem: [Printed in the Syrisches Waisenhaus].

Steegmuller, F. (ed.) (1972), *Flaubert in Egypt: A Sensibility on Tour. A Narrative drawn from Gustave Flaubert's Travel Notes & Letters*. Boston: Little, Brown.

Stone, W. (1884) *Shall We Annex Egypt?* London: Sampson Low, Marston, Searle and Rivington.

Storrs, Sir R. (1937), *Orientations*. London: I. Nicholson & Watson.

Taylor, A. and Taylor, L. (1964), 'A reminiscence of Lawrence: the story of Fareedah Akle'. *Viewpoints*, 4 (9), 22–4.

Taylor, J., Leach, B. and Sharp, H. (2011), 'The history and conservation of the papyrus of Tuy'. *The British Museum Technical Research Bulletin*, 5, 95–104.

T. E. Lawrence Studies (2012), www.telstudies.org (accessed 22 December 2013).

Thackeray, W. M. (1846), *Notes of a journey from Cornhill to Grand Cairo, by way of Lisbon, Athens, Constantinople, and Jerusalem: performed in the steamers of the Peninsular and oriental company* (Putnam's choice library). London: Chapman and Hall.

The Historical Magazine, and Notes and Queries Concerning the Antiquities, History, and Biography (1859), 'New York', 3.5, May, p. 146.

The Literary Gazette and Journal of the Belles-Lettres (1819), 'A Narrative of the Expedition to Algiers in 1816 &c. By M. A. Salamé', 267–77.

The Spectator (1863), 'Four months in a Dahabëeh', 8 June 1863, p. 18.

The Times (1874), 'Excursions to Egypt and Palestine', 9 June, p. 6.

Thimm C.A. (1898), *Egyptian Self-Taught (Arabic)* (Marlborough's self-taught series). London: E. Marlborough & Co.

Thomas, J. L. (1890), *Oxford to Palestine: Being Notes of a Tour made in the Autumn of 1889*. London: Leadenhall Press.

Thomas Cook, Ltd (1876a), *Cook's Tourists' Handbook for Egypt, the Nile and the desert*. London: Thomas Cook and Son.

—(1876b), *Cook's Tourists' Handbook for Palestine and Syria*. London: Thomas Cook and Son.

Traboulsi, F. (2009), 'Edward Said's Orientalism revisited: translations and translators'. *The Translator*, 15 (1), 179–83.

Twain, M. (1869), *The Innocents Abroad, or, The New Pilgrims' Progress*. Hartford, Conn.: American Publishing Company.

Van Ess, D. F. (1974), *Pioneers in the Arab World*, The Historical Series of the Reformed Church in America, no. 3. Grand Rapids, MI: Wm. B. Eerdmans Publishing Co.

Van Ess, J. (1917), *The Spoken Arabic of Mesopotamia*. Oxford: At the University Press.

Venuti, L. (2008), *The Translator's Invisibility: A History of Translation* (2nd edn). London: Routledge.

Walker, C. T. (1892), *A Colored Man Abroad: What He Saw and Heard in the Holy Land and Europe*. Augusta, GA: J. M. Weigle.

Walker, D. A. (1891), 'Summer Touring in the Holy Land'. *The Old and New Testament Student*, 12, 97–101.

Ward, W. H. (1885), 'The Wolfe Expedition', *Journal of the Society of Biblical Literature and Exegesis*, 5 (1/2): 56-60.

—(1886), 'Report on the Wolfe Expedition to Babylonia'. *Papers of the Archaeological Institute of America*, 5–33.

—(1898), 'A Portion of the Diary of William Hayes Ward, Director of the Wolfe Expedition to Babylonia (1884–85), Including Selections and Topographical Data from That Part of the Diary which Covers the Time Spent in Babylonia', in J. P. Peters, *Nippur or Explorations and Adventures on the Euphrates. The Narrative of the University of Pennsylvania Expedition to Babylonia in the years 1888–1890*. Vol. I: *First Campaign*. New York and London: G. P. Putnam's Sons, pp. 317–75.

—(1910), *The Seal Cylinders of Western Asia*. Washington, DC: The Carnegie Institution of Washington.

Warner, C. D. (1876), *My Winter on the Nile: Among the Mummies and Moslems*. Hartford, CT: American Pub. Co..

Waterfield, R. (1998), *Herodotus: The Histories* (Oxford World's Classics). Oxford: Oxford University Press.

Wilkinson, Sir G. (1847), *Hand-Book for Travellers in Egypt*. London: John Murray.

Winstone, H. V. F. (1990), *Woolley of Ur. The Life of Sir Leonard Woolley*. London: Secker & Warburg.

Wolff, P. (1857), *Arabischer Dragoman für Besucher des Heiligen Landes*. Leipzig: J. J. Weber.

Woolley, C. L. (1920), *Dead Towns and Living Men*. London: Humphrey Milford and
    Oxford University Press.
—(ed.) (1921), *From Kastamuni to Kedos, Being a Record of Experiences of Prisoners
    of War in Turkey, 1916–1918*. Oxford: Basil Blackwell.

Index

Adams Colony, Jaffa 114, 126
Ade, George 13, 28, 30, 34, 115
el Adlëéh, Mohamed (dragoman of Miss Carey) 23–4
Al-Akle, Fareedah 52–4, 132
Alexandria 15, 83, 113, 124
antiquities (trade in) 2, 7–9, 24, 50, 52, 56, 73–4, 76–7, 84, 90, 95–8, 100–4, 130, 133
Arabic language 1, 8, 10, 12, 15, 16, 26–7, 29, 31–44, 45–50, 52–5, 56–61, 65–70, 71, 80, 82–4, 104, 108, 110, 114, 120, 127, 129, 131, 132
   dialects 33, 36, 42, 43, 44, 48–9, 52–4
   difficulty or ease of learning 33, 36, 42–3, 48
   phrasebooks and grammars 31–43, 46, 48, 52, 65
archaeology and archaeologists 45–71
army
   British 36, 45, 54, 59, 60–4, 69, 110–12
   Ottoman 48, 64, 76, 78–9, 84
Aswan 31, 44

Babylon 12, 93–4, 98
Baghdad 55, 59, 73, 75, 84, 86, 89, 95
Bankes, William John 7
Beirut 17, 37, 43, 52, 106, 107, 108, 109, 113, 120
Bell, Gertrude 59–60
Belzoni, Giovanni 6
Bible 11–12, 33, 59, 68, 73, 80, 85, 99, 111, 115, 116, 133

Cairo 7–8, 17, 20, 21, 24, 30, 31, 32, 35, 43, 46, 48, 52, 60, 65, 92, 110–13, 117, 124
Carchemish 51, 52, 53, 55–7, 59, 66
Carey, M. L. M. 22–5

Christianity and Christians 3, 12, 71, 78, 79, 80, 87, 88, 89, 116, 117, 123
Christian missions and missionaries 34, 37, 52, 65, 70, 71, 73, 108, 109, 126, 132
Christie, Agatha 4, 64–71
   Appointment with Death 68, 71
   Death on the Nile 68
   Murder in Mesopotamia 67
Constantinople 1, 55, 60, 75, 76, 79, 81, 92, 98
Cook, Thomas (company) 1–2, 4, 31, 32, 36, 46, 113–14, 130
cuneiform tablets 46, 59, 73, 74, 76, 95–101

Dahoum (companion of T. E. Lawrence) 53, 132
Dalrymple, Lord 105–7, 125
Damascus 62, 82, 105, 131
D'Athanasi, Giovanni 'Yanni' 6–9, 130–1
dragoman
   ethnicities 9, 61–4, 75, 109
   meaning and etymology of term 2, 16
   as metaphor 37, 40
   qualities sought by clients 3, 17, 23, 27–9, 110, 114–17, 120–2, 124, 133
   training 16, 20–1, 70, 109, 110, 114–15, 119, 132
   travel without a dragoman 15–16, 46–8
   truthfulness 7, 29, 111
   'tyranny' of 13, 19–20, 22, 24, 124

eBay 6, 108
Eden, Mr and Mrs Frederic 4, 15, 16, 46
El Hani (dragoman) 114
espionage 13, 60

Finati, Giovanni 6–9

First World War 10, 60, 71, 126, 133, prisoner of war camps 59, 61–4
Flaubert, Gustave 2, 4, 26, 33
Floyd, Rolla 113–15, 117, 118, 125–6, 133

Gandour, Khalil S. 4, 5
Goddard, Sir Daniel Ford 117, 119
Goodknight, Ella L. 105–6
Greene, Ulysses W. 126–7
guidebooks 17, 19, 29, 31, 33, 35
    Baedeker 15–20, 28, 31–4, 46–7, 68, 130
    John Murray 17, 20, 23, 33, 46
    Shepheard's Hotel 32
    Thomas Cook 32

Haj Wahid (dragoman) 57–8
Hamoudi ibn Sheikh Ibrahim 66–7
Hanna Abu Sa'ab (dragoman) 30
Harfouch, Joseph 37, 39, 40
Hassam, A. 36, 37, 43, 52
Hassan (dragoman) 29
Herodotus, and his dragoman 12, 13, 16, 28, 62
Hilprecht, Hermann V. 73, 74, 75, 80, 81, 87, 89, 99–101, 129, 131, 132

interpreters and interpreting
    invisibility 3, 10–11, 75, 89, 91, 105,
    varied roles 1–2, 13, 28, 57–8, 77, 88, 121

Jaffa 4, 17, 113, 114, 120, 121, 126, 127
Jerusalem 7, 17, 20, 21, 30, 43, 68, 105, 108, 111, 113, 114, 124, 125, 126, 127, 129, 133
Joseph (dragoman of Gustave Flaubert) 26

Kastamuni 59, 61–4
Kedos 59, 61, 62
Kelly, Robert Talbot 35, 43
Koehler, Edna 126–7
Kuchuk Hanem 2–3

Latter Day Saints, Reorganized Church of Jesus Christ of (RLDS) 126
Lawrence, T. E. 4, 36, 50–5, 57, 132
Luxor 8, 24, 30, 31, 45

Mahmoud (dragoman of George Ade) 30–1, 115
Mahmoud (fictional dragoman in *Appointment with Death*) 68–70, 71
Mallowan, Sir Max 4, 59, 64–7, 69, 71
Miller, Ellen E. 109–10, 112, 120–4, 125
al-Miṣrī, Khalīfah ibn Maḥmūd 40–1
Moursi Ali (dragoman of J. L. Thomas) 124
Mousa, Suleiman 54
museums
    British Museum 55, 56, 58, 59, 60, 76
    Imperial Museum (Constantinople) 98
    Louvre 98
    Metropolitan Museum of Art (New York) 76, 96, 97, 98
    Museum of Fine Arts (Boston) 95
    Philadelphia Museum of Art 102
    University of Pennsylvania Museum 99, 100

Nakhlah, Yacoub 35–6, 39
Negima, Olinda 'Lulu' 108, 126–7
Negima, Solomon N. 6, 8, 20, 40, 105–27, 133
Newark, New Jersey 91, 92, 94, 95, 103
Nile Expedition (1884–5) 110–13
Nippur 6, 80, 83, 84–8, 90, 91, 92, 94, 97, 99
Noorian, Daniel Z. 6, 8, 9, 75, 77, 78, 79, 80, 81, 82, 83, 84, 85, 86, 87, 88, 89, 90, 91–104, 133, 134

Odeh, Rev. Naser 36, 37, 52, 132
Orientalism and Orientalist depictions of the Near East 2, 11, 16, 25, 115, 121, 125, 130
Ottoman Empire, authorities 55–7, 64, 82, 88, 131

Pennsylvania, University of 59, 73, 77, 80, 89, 97, 99–100
    Babylonian Expedition 77, 80–90, 91, 92, 97
Peters, John 77, 80–90, 97, 99–101, 103
Petrie, W. M. Flinders 3–4, 36, 45–50, 51, 54, 132
pyramids 12, 22, 28

Said, Edward 1–2, 10, 21
Salamé, Abraham V. 3
Salt, Henry 8–9
souvenirs, shopping and bargaining
        12–13, 17, 22, 24, 27, 34, 39,
        116–17
Stone, William 112, 117

testimonial letters, of dragomans 6, 13,
        21, 31, 40, 105–12, 115–17, 121,
        124–5, 127
Thackeray, W. M. 4, 21–2
Thebes *see* Luxor
Thomas, Rev. Joseph Llewellyn 109, 120,
        124
travel writing (as a literary genre) 2, 21–5
Turkish language 1, 8, 40, 48, 55, 57, 58,
        61, 62, 65, 75, 78, 79, 80, 81, 82, 83,
        84, 103, 104, 131, 132

Twain, Mark 21, 26, 106, 114

Ur 59, 65, 66, 67, 70

Van Ess, John 65–7

Walker, Rev Charles T. 117, 118, 124
Walker, Dean A. 4, 15
Ward, Rev William Hayes 73–80, 83,
        90, 91, 92, 93, 94, 95, 97, 98, 100,
        104
Warner, Charles Dudley 26, 27
Wolfe Expedition 73–80, 81, 83, 90, 91,
        95, 97, 133
women travellers 22–5, 29, 37, 69, 108,
        120–4
Woolley, Sir Leonard 4, 53, 54–64, 65, 66,
        132
Woolley, Katharine 67, 70

www.ingramcontent.com/pod-product-compliance
Lightning Source LLC
Chambersburg PA
CBHW062037270326
41929CB00014B/2461